To Fiona,
Blessed Be! Col x

Deferred

Illuminating W
Darker Times

Practical Coping Strategies
learned in an autistic life

Katherine Highland

ISBN 978-1-326-67871-5

Author's Note:
The decision was made to illustrate this book in black and white to lower printing costs. The original drawings were in colour and more effective but would have meant a much higher price. The priority was to make the book as affordable and thereby accessible as it can be.

Contents

Introduction

The guides, strategies and advice in this book are written from my own experience; I have some personal history of all issues covered. Situations and people all differ; these are guidelines to add to your own judgement and support.

I am in my 40s at the time of writing and was diagnosed autistic in January 2008 at the age of 35. In 2012 I moved from Edinburgh to the Scottish Highlands; I was already involved with Autism Initiatives as a service user and volunteer at Number 6 in Edinburgh and I now have the same roles at the Highland one stop shop, which is based in Inverness and works across the Highlands. This is the second publication I have written as part of my work and wish to reach out and help others who are going through similar events and crises to those I have faced. I have not fully experienced every scenario mentioned, for instance I have never travelled abroad nor have I been in trouble with the police. I have used a combination of logic and what I have learned from talking to or reading about others in similar situations to expand my advice on some scenarios.

I have written this book under a pen-name because my elderly parents, who do not live in the Highlands, are unaware of my diagnosis and some of the personal history I mention would cause them considerable distress. I am nonetheless proud to be a part of the autistic community and it is important to me to celebrate the positive aspects of being autistic, even during the difficult times. I take particular pleasure when writing these coping strategies in looking at ways in which we can make our autistic traits work in our favour; challenging the assumption often still found in society that all aspects of a disability must be negative and restrictive.

Another positive aspect of coping which has been very important to me is finding the funny, warm and unexpectedly uplifting sides to situations, even the most painful. It is my belief that advice is easier to relate to when it is accompanied by a personal touch; a funny story, a special moment, a very individual autistic slant on a hard earned positive outcome. I have therefore included some of these in the chapter introductions.

As I thought about what title I could give this book and looked through my photos for inspiration, it occurred to me that my solar garden lights could be seen to represent what I am trying to achieve here. They store up the sun's light and energy, bringing it out when it's needed. Whatever your reasons for reading this, I thank you for your interest; may you walk in starlight whenever life is cold and dark and your path is hard going.

Blessed Be,

Kat Highland

Looking forward

There must be lots more ideas and strategies out there that I haven't thought of. I hope that my own experiences, cautionary tales and solutions will help others but at the same time I respect and appreciate the wealth of other autistic input available. My colleagues and fellow autistic people would love to hear from anyone who has advice of their own to add. As time goes on and others add their own contributions, perhaps one day we could have a sequel!

Please contact the Highland One Stop Shop or Autism Initiatives Scotland Head Office if you wish to share anything, or if you have any comments or questions for me. Contact details are on the back page of this book.

Chapter 1: Psychological Self Defence

The idea for writing the course on which this chapter is based came to me after going through the Late Diagnosis Group sessions at the Highland One Stop Shop. The sessions generated a lot of solidarity through people sharing personal experiences, sometimes for the first time after years of keeping them inside. One of the most important roles of the one stop shops is to provide a safe, completely autism friendly space where people can share things with others who will understand without the lengthy explanations we often have to give over and over again in the rest of the world. Time after time the relief in the room was palpable as people including me shared stories which were instantly identified with by the others. I decided to put something together which would take this one stage further; to build on the sharing and expressing of these situations and the feelings they invoke. I wanted to use my existing background in writing coping strategies to help people plan out techniques to cope and make things better for themselves when similar events occurred in the future.

Autistic people can be strongly affected by situations and incidents which barely register with others. Something as apparently trivial as getting someone's name wrong, being jostled in a shop and tutted at or dropping a bus pass in a queue can bother us for the rest of the day or even longer and keep on popping back into our memory. It is one of the more difficult aspects of being autistic that we often have issues with things like hand-eye coordination, manual dexterity, cognitive processing speed, memory and concentration. These things as well as sensory overload make us more vulnerable to those everyday technical hitches that embarrass, frustrate and unsettle us so much.

It can even overshadow the skills and talents we have. We tend not to be very good at giving ourselves a break. We try too hard to please people in our quest for connection and inclusion. As our own autism knowledge and self awareness increase, we need to get better at saying "no" appropriately. This gives us more to think about and work on even as some things may be getting easier.

Then when you add the complications and exhaustion of social interaction, you begin to see why we struggle so much at times; why we can be mistakenly thought to be aloof, slow or emotionless. Emotionless? As if! Anyone who has watched coverage of Wimbledon, even catching it when changing channels, will be familiar with the grunts of exertion for which professional tennis players are notorious. The effort put into each shot is visible as well as audible. For autistic people, keeping up our side of a conversation can require just as much mental energy, especially when it's more than a simple to and fro with one person on the other side of the net. We have to deal with every smash, ace and backhand from all directions. There is no umpire to regulate the amplified background distractions we experience either, nor any fleet-footed ball boy or girl to keep us supplied with words to volley. Our exertion is silent; there is no outward cue to show the people around us how hard we are having to work.

All of these challenges build up to fatigue, depression and feeling overwhelmed. I know these feelings and I am forever grateful for the existence of the Late Diagnosis Group for providing the framework in which my idea grew. I still recall the moment the title "psychological self defence" came into my mind; it was a grey Wednesday morning as I walked along Grampian Road in Aviemore to one of my voluntary jobs. Once I had looked it up online to check that nobody else had a course with that name, the structure and content began to come together. I have learned from every group to whom I have delivered the course and I shall continue to learn from every future one.

Psychological Self Defence

This chapter is adapted from a course I wrote and deliver to autistic people. It aims to help us all find ways to cope better with everyday stressful situations which affect confidence and self esteem. The first session is understanding our basic psychological needs as human beings and how autism enhances and adds to those needs. The second session looks at why everyday stressful situations can be extra hard to cope with. The third session looks at ways to use the positive traits of autism to our advantage in coping with situations and how we feel. The final session is for looking at ways to cope when things go wrong and developing a personalised coping plan to refer to quickly and easily when needed. Many of the principles in the course are relevant to topics covered throughout this book.

Overview of psychological needs

We can begin to deal with situations better once we understand more about why they are difficult. To understand this, we can start by understanding what we need, both as human beings and in terms of our autism.

General human needs include:

- To be safe, both physically and emotionally
- To have a sense of self worth and a purpose in the world around us
- To have reciprocal interaction (give and take, connect with others)
- To have and understand boundaries
- To keep well; maintain a healthy routine, preserve mental health and be able to manage stress
- To have validation, support and acknowledgement when things go wrong
- To feel in control of ourselves

- To have space to change our minds and to repair mistakes

Autism specific needs include:

The following quoted from “Autism and Mental Health: The Views of People on the Autistic Spectrum on Their Mental Health Needs and Mental Health Services", March 2011 Written by Autism Rights Group Highland (ARGH) and Highland User Group (HUG), to view the whole text please see:

www.arghighland.co.uk/pdf/arghhug.pdf

“Locally, in March 2011 the Autistic people’s organisation ARGH (Autism Rights Group Highland) described some of their needs. To -

- Feel secure, safe and understood.
- Be fulfilled and have a sense of achievement.
- Have relationships and social contact with other people on the autistic spectrum.
- Be valued, have our strengths acknowledged.
- Have somewhere we feel at ease and protected in.
- Feel that we are not broken or wrong or bad.
- Feel valued in society and at work and school.
- Have stability, control and order in our lives.
- Have peace and calm.
- Be accepted for who we are with an understanding that Autism is a way of being not a lifestyle choice.”

Several of these needs overlap and this illustrates that autistic people are very much part of the wider community of human beings.

Reasons why autism can make situations more difficult

- It is an "invisible" condition. People do not know to make allowances or the appropriate adjustments, though a vague, indefinable vulnerability is often associated with autistic people.

- Many autistic people tend to lack confidence because of past experiences, long term struggles and the same things seeming to go wrong over and over again.

- Difficulty reading people is often a feature of autism and this can lead to misunderstandings when it is not clear how someone else feels.

- Sensory issues can add to difficulties because they make the world a very hectic and tiring place for us, giving a lot to think about and try to take in, including what to many non-autistic people is just in the background and not even noticed.

- Fatigue makes us extra sensitive, vulnerable and unable to react quickly. This in turn leads to panic and feelings of being overwhelmed.

- Trouble processing situations in real time (as they are happening, i.e. "live"). We need extra time to think through everything that is going on, whether or not it is part of the situation itself.

- Face blindness (not recognising people immediately, or at all, out of context; a lifetime of the unintentional offence and misunderstandings this causes can have an enormous cumulative effect on our sense of security).

- Speech and behaviour patterns can be distinctive and open to misinterpretation. We can come across as formal or abrupt when we do not mean to be. Either we don't realise, or we are suffering inside because we realise just too late that we have "done it again".

- Overthinking and overanalysing; being permanently on the defensive. This can make us see problems or hostility in a situation or an encounter with someone when in fact we are mistaken. We then react in a way which the other people involved don't expect or understand.

- Literal interpretation of what others say, including "feeling" the literal meaning even when we understand the intended meaning.

- Intensity and long duration of feelings / emotions (the "will this be as important in five years time" philosophy is not generally helpful to autistic people; we need to manage what is tremendously important now. It will be just as important for the rest of the day or week and still just as important next time we have to go to the same place or deal with the same people.)

- Projecting our own logical, deep thinking onto others, ie sometimes we give too much credit to people who don't think things through as we would, or who make behaviour choices we would not make. Autistic people do have empathy, but one thing we struggle to empathise with is lack of empathy in others.

Skills and techniques to develop and use

- Knowledge (understanding why something is difficult as opposed to wondering "why am I not coping better?")

- Damage limitation (prioritising our own safety, peace of mind and not making situations worse, rather than trying to win or get the last word.)

- Disclosure of autism; appropriate or not? (Including use of autism alert cards. It is not safe or advisable with ignorant, drunk or aggressive strangers but beneficial in more official circumstances such as police questions or comparatively low level scenarios such as a shop assistant becoming impatient.)

- Question negative thoughts and assumptions (this is very difficult for autistic people but it can be helpful to stop and think whether we are seeing problems or hostile intentions that aren't there.)

- Manage the moment, then prepare for the future (avoid reactions including use of language which could get you into trouble; use the prospect of having to face a person or place again as an incentive to cut short a situation and curb your reaction.)

- Process the situation in the right place at the right time (get to a safe, non public place and put the situation away in your mind until then; avoid being so consumed by it that you walk straight into another confrontation or put yourself in danger through losing awareness of traffic etc.)

- Accept that sometimes you will not be able to figure it all out (understanding how and why a situation happened, down to the fine details on a scientific level, can be very important to our comfort and security; staying in a situation to ask people why they do or say things is often unwise as it exposes your vulnerability.)

- Make your autism work in your favour (use the traits to positive effect. Use the urge to do the right thing to control reactions. Use rigidity of your own rules to set yourself limits and walk away or to avoid potential flashpoints such as mentioning subjects or people you know make someone else angry. Use the tendency to seek quiet space to allow yourself to leave a bad situation rather than make it worse.)

- Know what you can control (your own actions but not other people's.)

- Acknowledge that seeking the right help is a form of keeping control (report harassment and other criminal behaviour; talk to autism support staff, GP etc about problems coping; confide in friends and family.)

Coping after something goes wrong and planning a strategy

After a situation has happened:

- See the funny side (it can be very difficult and take a long time but it really helps.)

- Be aware of thinking about it too much (replaying it over and over with the outcome you wanted; speculating why it went wrong. This is called ruminating.)

- Accept that others make mistakes or do not have your high standards.

- Share the experience and get support (from trusted people; strangers, including people you only know online, can appear sympathetic but take advantage.)

- Restore your self esteem (remember and refer to things you have done well; skills others involved in the situation would not have, times you handled challenges well.)

- Accept that some times you will cope better than others (feeling you have not handled something as well as you handled something similar in the past doesn't mean you have failed or lost the progress you have made.)

- Never, ever turn feelings of frustration and powerlessness on someone else who seems weaker. This is bullying and if the temptation to do so becomes more than a passing thought, help is urgently needed. This doesn't mean snapping at the wrong person in the heat of the moment. Everyone, autistic or not, has done that. The danger is deliberately taking frustration out on someone because you can get away with it. Everyone has bad thoughts sometimes, but if you cannot stop yourself turning them into harmful behaviour, you must be honest and seek help.

Planning a personalised strategy:

The plan is in three sections and involves making a few notes in each. The sections are:

1. What makes situations especially difficult for you;

2. Some simple guidelines to read over and use to help you;

3. Some positive thoughts to look at after something has upset you.

You can make up your own plan and it could be helpful to personalise it even more by decorating it with your favourite colours, song lyrics, quotes that inspire you, stickers, scraps of material in textures that comfort you, drawings, anything at all. The headings for the three sections are a starting point for you to write your own reminders:

1. I must give myself a break and remember that the down side of my autism makes some situations harder to cope with because:

2. When a situation makes me frustrated, stressed or upset, I will try to:

3. Sometimes things will still go wrong. When I feel bad, I must remember:

Your reminders will be appropriate to your own difficulties. We are all different; some of us struggle with things others find less of a problem. These are some examples of the kind of things you might write.

For point 1:

I cannot always hear properly what people say when the environment is noisy.

I am tired a lot and this makes me feel irritable and slow to take things in.

My speech is sometimes very formal when people don't expect it.

For point 2:

Remember that taking longer to absorb what people say is overload, not stupidity.

Focus on getting out of the situation with dignity, not trying to win, because my peace of mind is more important and I do not need the stress of worrying about the next time I have to see someone after a big argument.

Remember that this is NOT the same as [a bad situation from the past].

For point 3:

I did really well when I [describe a situation you coped with well or a time you did something you are proud of] and nothing can ever take that away from me.

Not everybody has high standards or treats people with respect as I do; I should be proud of how hard I try even when it is exasperating that others seem not to.

Other people make mistakes too, even when they seem confident and successful.

Chapter 2: Festivals and Crowded Events

This chapter was originally written when I lived in Edinburgh, to help service users at Number 6 to cope with the Festival. This is a particularly long period of extra crowds and disruption to familiar routines and surroundings which, although very rich, interesting and positive for the economy and international reputation of the Scottish capital, has specific challenges for autistic people living and working in and around the city. I was never against the Festival as such; I appreciated its value and went to some interesting events. I would have missed it if it had stopped happening every August. I did find it tiring and stressful though, and I knew that a lot of my fellow service users would be feeling the same.

The best thing about the Festival for me was how it enhanced my love of September. It has always felt like a coming alive month to me; a time for new beginnings as the air sharpens, cools and freshens and colours start to come out after the long green days of July and August. By the time September comes around, I am always ready for the new season; the long daylight is beginning to feel overloading and intrusive. I look forward to being out when the streetlights are on again; to solar lights in the garden coming on early enough to sit outside and enjoy them and to fairy lights and warm spice scented candles indoors. In Edinburgh it is the month when the city can breathe again as the crowds disperse. I wondered if I would lose much of that rejuvenation when I moved to Aviemore; much as I was glad not to have to deal with the Festival any more, I wondered if I would miss that dramatic change. However, August is still a busy month here, as is July so the end of the English school holidays still makes a difference.

Besides, the comfortingly inexorable progress of the seasons and the variation in the daylight hours are even more distinct here, blessed as Aviemore is with a mountain skyline on both sides.

I have kept the Edinburgh Festival in this chapter as a case study, since it is of such long duration. The general principles can be applied to any crowded event. Much of the advice can be applied to anyone visiting a place at the same time as a big event, whether or not that is the purpose of their trip, as well as to people coping with events in their home town.

Rainbow over Calton Hill, Edinburgh

Festivals and Crowded Events

Getting ready

It is useful to begin by understanding why it is so stressful when these events disrupt routine. Knowing why something is different is an important first step towards coping with it. Most modern towns and cities were built many hundreds of years ago to accommodate a much smaller permanent population than they have now, never mind the large numbers of people who come to stay when there is a special event. When these events happen regularly, for example at a particular time every year, they grow over the years as they become well known but there is still only so much space in the host town or city. We also have to consider that the nature of many of these events means a lot of the people coming to them will be very flamboyant, excitable and happy to be in a crowded situation; there are also people from the media here to report on what is happening for those who are interested but cannot be there. When you look at it this way, the fact that everywhere is suddenly so busy makes more sense.

The next step towards making the time of disruption run as smoothly as possible is accepting that during that time, things will be different. Streets, shops and buses will be more crowded; traffic heavier; routine journeys will take longer. Allow more time for all journeys and anything which involves you being where the crowds are. As far as possible, try to do what you can in advance to save you having to come into town or stay for longer than necessary. Some ways in which you can do this may be:

- Buy presents in advance for any birthdays or other occasions the dates of which fall at the affected time.
- Stock up on non perishable foods so that you have less to buy and carry if you shop in town.
- Try to arrange appointments for before or after; if necessary explain that it is difficult for you to deal with

the crowds at this time due to your condition and get a support worker to back you or go with you.

- If you use taxis, remember that they will be more in demand than usual and you will need to book in advance for any essential journeys when you have to be somewhere on time.
- Find out whether regular appointments such as counselling may be changed to somewhere easier for you to get to and from during the affected time; this may need a few weeks' notice to be arranged.

Talk to your support workers in advance if you are concerned, whether about coping generally or about a specific task you have to do or journey you have to make during the affected time. The stress created by extra crowds is a legitimate issue and your concerns will be taken seriously. It may be useful for you to find out about and start practising some relaxation and breathing exercises so that you will know what to do if you need to use them. Your support worker or GP can advise you about this or you could look up relaxation techniques online. If you work, variations to your start and finish times or a quiet space to unwind may be considered as a reasonable adjustment. Get your support workers to back you up and ask in good time.

Check in advance whether your bus is expected to be diverted at any time. Bus companies have such information on their websites; local papers and radio are excellent sources of up to date information on diversions and road closures as well as advice on how you can get to where you need to be. Remember though that sometimes things can still happen which cause diversions at short notice.

Try to keep an open mind to the possibility that the event does not have to be an all negative experience just to be coped with; remind yourself of the benefits to the local economy and the fact that it makes so many people want to come to the town or city. If it is your home town, they have to go away again and you get to live in the area; many of them will be very envious! There can be a nice warm feeling amongst locals of all being in it together having a good-natured moan about the chaos; sometimes people complain about something but quite enjoy having it to talk about and look forward to the time when everything becomes more peaceful again. There may be shows or events which interest you; look at guides to what is coming up in local press and just see if there is anything which you may enjoy. Remember though that some shows may involve people being picked out from the audience and sometimes the performers will try very hard to persuade someone even if they say no. Ask at the box office whether there is any chance this may happen; you do not have to tell them why you are asking but make sure that you feel safe and are fully informed before buying a ticket. Always remember you have as much right as everyone else to make the best of the time; join in as much or as little as is comfortable for you.

During the event period

It is important that you feel sure of your own boundaries and how you will deal with strangers. There may be more people than usual handing out leaflets and asking passers by to come to their events and shows. The important thing to remember is balance. They are entitled to promote their show but not to block anyone's path or pester them once they have said no. If you are not interested or do not want to be approached, a polite "No, thank you" is all you need to say and you have every right to walk away. Most people will accept this and not say anything further to you; if you do encounter the small minority who are rude or persistent, it is they who are in the wrong and you need to look after yourself by getting out of that situation with minimal disruption to your own activities and your peace of mind. Trying to get the last word or score points over them for making a remark which offended you will make the situation escalate and you may well come off worse;

distressed, unsettled and even more afraid of the crowds. Part of living with invisible conditions such as autism is accepting that you have a condition which is not obvious to strangers and sometimes people can misunderstand you when they do not realise you are genuinely uncomfortable with their forward approach and why; they cannot see how you are feeling. It is best not to try to explain in such situations, especially in public. You do not owe them any explanation and if you reveal your condition they may react with further rudeness or ask questions which you may not feel able to answer. The safest and most victorious thing you can do is to walk away. You are never obliged to have a conversation with someone you do not know, unless they are police, stewards or someone in authority giving necessary instructions; even in that case, you are not obliged to chat socially and they are obliged to be courteous and professional. You can always say that you have to go; you do not have to say where or why. It is no-one else's business and it is a true thing to say even if you are not really busy or needing to get somewhere on time; if you are uncomfortable and need to leave the situation, then you have to go.

If you are asked for directions and do not know the answer or find yourself unable to remember it clearly, just say that you do not know; there will always be lots of other people they can ask. It is perfectly natural in such situations that even if you are asked about a place where you have been before, you may find it difficult to put the information together when "put on the spot". This is all part of your condition and it is not a lie to say that you are not sure; it is true in the circumstances and an acceptable way to avoid making the other person feel awkward for having asked you. Alternatively, you may feel more confident if you carry an up to date street map with you. It could help you not only when actually asked for directions but by making you feel calmer because you are prepared.

Be realistic and allow yourself to adapt your usual routines. You may want to consider meeting friends somewhere different for the affected period if you usually meet them in the city centre; meet in one another's homes or look for quieter places out of town, or wait until the event is over and keep in touch by phone, text, email, the social networking sites you normally use or whichever means you have available. It is not giving in to do this; it is adapting for a time to circumstances which you cannot control. True friends will understand this and support you; be honest about why you need to do things differently for a few weeks. The fact is that there are a lot more people around for the time the event is running and regular haunts will be more crowded and noisy than they normally are; it is likely to be difficult to have a conversation and your friends may well be just as keen as you are to go somewhere quieter! If you are going out in the city centre (and if you want to, there is no reason why you cannot), early in the day when the buses may be quieter you should bear in mind that if you usually sit in the front seats, people may well sit beside you even if there are a lot of double seats free so that they can look out for landmarks to tell them when to get off. If this makes you uncomfortable, consider sitting in the middle during the busy period as large noisy groups often head for the back seats. If the event is a festival, remember that late evening buses are likely to be especially busy and people may well be drunk and loud or argumentative; taxis will be difficult to get. The key is to do only what you feel comfortable doing and to keep yourself safe.

Dress in clothes which make you feel physically and psychologically comfortable. You need to be as relaxed as possible. You will see a lot of people in costume during festivals and carnivals. This can be turned into a positive way to distract yourself from the stress of being out and about; look out for unusual and colourful outfits. Remember though that even if someone is dressed in a deliberately distinctive way, it is considered bad etiquette to stare too openly or for too long when they are not actually performing for an audience. Once you have noticed them, keep on looking around for other interesting sights.

You may wish to make some notes of your own to fit any event you need to prepare for.

Try adding them to your phone, or write them on sticky notes and keep them in this book if you have the paperback version.

Planning for longer disruptions week by week: Case study (The Edinburgh Festival)

The Edinburgh Festival period lasts for four weeks every summer and is one of the longer regular crowd drawing events associated with a British city. This chapter was originally written specifically as a guide to coping with it for autistic people who are service users at Number 6 in Edinburgh. Many of these tips can be applied to events in other towns and cities.

You may find it helpful to have strategies in mind to help you to cope with the upheaval of Festival time and dividing it up into a week by week plan could help to break up the month. Although the dates vary and the city is busier from late July, generally the busiest time is the four week period which starts in whichever week has more days of August than July. These are just ideas to help you to get started; pick and choose, begin any stage at any time. It is your Festival time in your city; the aim is to make it work for you.

Week 1

Now is a good time to observe. Find out which routes, shops and public places are quieter than others and where you feel most comfortable and safe. These will not become obvious until the Festival is underway so use the techniques which you have prepared and take notice of what goes well. It should make you feel more in control and positive about the coming weeks.

Week 2

This could be a good time to focus your attention on finding places to go outside of the city centre where it will not be so crowded. Get a friend to go with you or arrange to meet with your support worker if this is practical; never take risks with your personal safety for the sake of going somewhere quiet. Although lonely places will seem more attractive during Festival time, remember that they can still have dangers of their own. If you are taking a trip to one of the small towns or villages served by your usual buses and walking around somewhere you do not know, it is better to go into a cafe or other family friendly venue than an unfamiliar pub especially if you are alone. If you find somewhere you like, you can always go back again throughout the Festival and beyond.

Week 3

You will probably be very tired by now so think about focusing on something you can do at home. Make time and space to practice your relaxation and breathing techniques, even just for a few minutes; set aside a quiet, restful area and set it up to be an enjoyable exercise, perhaps with a soothing CD or set of wind chimes. August tends to bring a lot of hot and humid weather so lighting candles may not work so well; a colour changing lamp or ornament, widely available nowadays in many shops, may be more suitable.

Week 4

The time has come to start looking forward to the return to normality. Take time to give yourself a treat or reward for having coped so far and enjoy thinking about and planning the things you will feel more comfortable doing again; the places you will go to as you did before. Start planning and enjoy making the necessary contact to pick up on any social routines which you had put on hold.

Notes to make

Write down the contact details you need for your own circumstances; your bus company, local taxi firms, Festival events which interest you and the telephone numbers or website details for any new places about which you would like to find out more as part of your search for less crowded venues.

Chapter 3: Working

At the time of my diagnosis I was working full time in a large office in Edinburgh. It was an open plan layout over two floors in an eleven storey building with a communal canteen. I worked with good, decent, friendly people but it was a sensory nightmare! The very complex social structure and the frequently bitty, changeable and inconsistent nature of the workload were extremely difficult especially before I knew about my autism and how it affects me. I became very unhappy and isolated, largely due to fatigue and social barriers as do so many autistic people in the workplace especially when we don't know about our condition.

Naturally, I spent as much time getting away to the Highlands as I possibly could! I worked flexi-time and since I was so generally unhappy, I went by the philosophy that any day I had to go to work was a day written off so I may as well work long hours in order to save up for more days when I didn't wake up with that to face. With hindsight I can see that I was storing up trouble as well as flexi credit; I made myself even more tired and neglected the rest of my life. I was encouraging myself to feel negatively about my time at work. I do however stand by the feeling of any day I worked being taken up entirely with that. I had no energy left by the time I got home even after a standard length working day. It was all I could do to get myself a decent nourishing dinner and keep up with essential housework. I thought that was just the way it had to be; I had no idea how people managed to go out socially on a weeknight and function the next day, even without alcohol being involved, or how they could go home and interact with their families or flatmates.

Bizarrely as it seemed at the time, I really enjoyed Sunday overtime. I could get through more work than I ever managed on a weekday. My bosses thought it was all about the money being an incentive. So did I; it got me on the Highland Chieftain to Inverness on a regular basis, in First Class too away from the crowds. I realise now that it wasn't just greed. I thrived on Sunday overtime because the phones weren't ringing and I got to tackle one particular paperwork based job consistently without getting halfway through my preparations and being asked to abandon the task and do something else! My grandfather used to say you got put in the moon if you worked on a Sunday. I told an elderly customer's daughter that one day when she phoned to check the authenticity of a call her mother had received from someone working overtime. It brightened up the day for both of us. Those moments were everything.

That was my only mainstream, full time and paid job, which I held for eleven years before my health went downhill. I made some lifelong friends and learned a lot. I am now fortunate enough to be getting the support I need, including benefits, to work much more productively in my office based but still varied volunteering roles with Autism Initiatives and the Strathspey Steam Railway. I deeply admire all of those autistic people who are managing to sustain employment in all kinds of jobs, some of which are in noisy, pressured and demanding environments. We all have our abilities and our limits; it is a matter of finding them and doing the best each of us can. We are all so different, comparing ourselves or being compared by others to other autistic people can become a further drain on us. We need to educate and remind ourselves as well as non-autistic people just how diverse we all are.

Working

This includes voluntary, supported and therapeutic work. There are a lot of good things about having a job; routine and structure, a sense of purpose and achievement, gaining skills and confidence. At the same time, the workplace can be a complex and pressured environment for autistic people and we need to have a coping plan in place. This will help us not only to get through the working day but to have a chance of enjoying it more.

Doing your job

Be aware of your own limits and make that awareness into something that is helpful to you. Recognise how fatigue, sensory overload, needing more time to process your thoughts and so on affect you. It is very important that you also recognise what aspects of doing your job work well for you. Nobody enjoys every task they have to do at work. You will, however, begin to notice that particular ways of working or surroundings bring out the best of your talents. It may be organising your workload a certain way; it may be getting an earlier start so that you can get certain tasks done or get your mind fully focused before phones start ringing or there are more people around. It may help you if you make notes of what goes well or not so well for you and why, or talk to someone in your support network and let them keep a note of it. This will help you to talk to your employer and colleagues about what reasonable adjustments you need. Think of this as helping them to help you; helping them to make the most of all you have to offer.

Whether you prefer to think of your being autistic as a disability, a condition or just the way it is, autism qualifies as a disability under equality laws. You are entitled to reasonable adjustments to help you to stay in work without your health suffering. If your employer does not let you or anyone acting as an advocate for you talk with them about your needs and look at what is possible with goodwill and common sense, they are breaking the law. It may not be possible to make all the adjustments you would need for an ideal working life, but there will be things that can be done to help you at work. Even small adjustments can make a big difference. If you give examples of what works well for you as well as what is difficult and why, it will help your employer to work out how to make things easier for you. It will also show them that you really want to do well at your job and it will give you a feeling of satisfaction that you are taking control of your life.

Make sure you take the breaks you are supposed to. It is bad for your health if you don't and although you may think it makes you look hardworking, in fact many employers frown upon people not taking their breaks. It can be very tempting to keep working because you don't want to lose focus and have to start again; remember that breaks are set and encouraged for a reason. It is also a good idea to spread out your holiday entitlement evenly so that you can recharge regularly and feel less unsettled coming back.

If you have the option of flexible working hours, this can be very useful. At the same time, be careful that you do not become too focused and tire yourself out. Like not taking breaks, building up too much flexi credit (or whatever your employer calls it when you have worked more hours than the standard working day) can become something you are spoken to about and asked to change. This can feel very upsetting and demoralising. There can be other problems too in that your job may not be covered when you are taking days off to use up hours you have already worked, so you could come back to a very daunting build-up. When this happens, it can easily lead to a destructive pattern of working long hours again to catch up, eventually becoming exhausted or being told you have to work set hours. The tendency of the autistic brain to focus on a task and lose awareness of time and other things that need attention means that flexible working hours have to be managed very carefully.

There may still be times when you cannot cope and need to take time off, whether because of problems associated with your autism or other health issues that arise. Everyone gets ill sometimes; people who go through their whole working lives without having to take sick leave are very rare and very lucky. Most companies have a policy on absence and it is important that you cooperate fully; keep your employer informed, make contact when agreed and provide any paperwork they ask for from you or your doctor. Proper management of sick leave should be focused on helping you to plan your return to work and to stay well. If you feel that this is not happening, seek help and advice from your union or your supporting professionals.

Making a positive difference

If your job involves helping or serving customers or clients, remember that you cannot make them your friends. It is good to make an effort to treat them as individuals, to be pleasant and polite and to take the trouble to think about ways to help in more complicated cases; this is sometimes called "going the extra mile". Empathy and compassion are often heightened in autistic people and make us vulnerable to becoming emotionally involved in our work, especially when we see people struggling with the same kind of things we do. However, you must never be tempted or pressured into bending or breaking the rules for a customer because you feel sorry for them. This can get you into a lot of trouble, get you suspended or even sacked. You cannot help that customer or any other if you are stopped from doing your job because you are in trouble; it will also cause you a huge amount of worry and distress. If you are thinking of doing something outside the usual things you do in your job to help a customer and you are not sure whether it is allowed, ask your supervisor or a trusted colleague and follow their guidance. If you need to confide in someone who supports you but is not part of the company you work for, make sure you do not tell them anything which would identify your customer or break confidentiality rules.

If you have an idea for doing something better or solving a problem, write it down and keep a copy with your name and the date. Some workplaces have a staff suggestions scheme; you may want to discuss it with a colleague you trust or show it to your supervisor or mentor before making it any more formal. Many autistic people think very creatively but can be vulnerable to missing details and perspectives so that we come up with a lot of ideas which don't work or get the reaction we expect. This can be very hard to cope with especially when it happens more than once. You have the right to have your ideas listened to and discussed; if they are not going to work, you should still be taken seriously, thanked for your thought and effort and an explanation given of why the idea has not been accepted; your feelings should be acknowledged with respect and compassion. It may be that your ideas can be developed or adapted into a different form but you have still made a valuable contribution by starting the discussion. You will need to take extra care of your self esteem and peace of mind when these difficult and frustrating times come. Keep a note of the times when you do well; remember that many autistic or suspected autistic people including very famous ones had many setbacks in between the successes they became known for.

If you feel that something is going wrong or you don't agree with something and it has to do with people who are your bosses, you need to be very careful how you approach it. You do not have to like your superiors or think the same way as they seem to, but you do have to respect their position. If you want to ask questions, do not do it in front of others, especially customers or the public. If you do not know the person well, it is best to seek the advice of someone you trust before approaching them. If you are aware beyond any doubt of something which is unquestionably wrong such as stealing or bullying, it is vital that you confide in someone. Do not try to deal with it on your own and only trust people you know very well to support and advise you on what to do. If you do not have that trusting relationship with anyone at your workplace, talk to someone in your support network such as a support worker, doctor or counsellor, or contact an organisation such as your trade union, the Citizens' Advice Bureau or The Samaritans who will often have useful contacts to advise you practically and help you with the stress.

Your working environment

There is more to staying productive and happy in your job than the work itself. Pay attention to what is good and bad for you in the place where you do your job. You may find that difficulties only become obvious when you look back on something you used to do in the past. Learning about difficulties other autistic people have had can be a powerful trigger of awareness; talk to other autistic people, read articles, books and posts about working on autism message boards. Think about all of your senses; sounds, lighting, smells, clutter, space, colours, traffic, echoes, distractions outside. You can then use this awareness to work with your employers on a plan of reasonable adjustments, just as you can do this about ways of doing your work.

Look into what in-work support is available to you. Your employer is legally bound to help you to access this support. Your trade union can advise on this and your autism support service, GP, support worker or any other care professional should have or be able to research contacts for you. Autistic run user groups, support groups and campaigning organisations in your area or nationally will also have access to contacts. It is important that you keep your GP informed about any difficulties you are having so that your medical notes are kept up to date and can be used to support and back you up if you need to claim any kind of help in future.

Interacting with people

This can be the most complex and difficult aspect of successful working for many autistic people. One of the first things you will have to consider and make decisions about is who to tell about your autism and when. This applies whether you take a job knowing you are autistic or are diagnosed while already in a job.

Understanding of autism is increasing but there will always be people who do not react in the way we would expect or like. This doesn't just mean negative reactions; people are sometimes too afraid of doing or saying the wrong thing so they appear to push us away, or they try too hard and make us feel awkward, underestimated or patronised. In many cases, patience, honesty, active listening and time invested by both sides will break down those barriers. It is helpful to encourage people to ask you questions; they may otherwise be afraid of offending you and try to guess what you need and how you feel. This can lead to misunderstandings.

There is no set rule for when you should disclose or to whom. This in itself is difficult; you need to acknowledge that and give yourself credit for the courage it takes every time you do disclose. As a guideline, it is advisable to disclose to someone at your workplace who is directly involved with setting your work, giving you feedback and making sure you are coping, and who is obliged to treat your personal information as confidential. Your employer is legally bound to help you and take your autism along with any other health problems into account but they cannot do this if they don't know about it. You can then work with this person on deciding whether to tell anyone else. If you do not feel that you can trust your immediate superiors, there will be other options; a trade union representative, a supervisor on another team or someone in a role which has to do with the welfare of people in the workplace. Some bigger companies have their own counselling and support services; this will often involve a telephone call but written contact could be considered as a reasonable adjustment.

Interacting with your colleagues over and above what is necessary to do your job is an inevitable part of working life and can add a lot of pleasure to your working day when it goes right. You don't always have to think of things to say; a smile and a "hello" can make a big difference and help to get friendly conversation started without you having to make all the effort. If you prefer to keep work completely separate from other parts of life, you have the right to do this but you should still be civil and treat others as you would like to be treated. You don't have to join in with chat or accept invitations to go out socially; you don't have to explain why you are saying no, but do so politely and thank your colleague for asking you. Being polite even if you don't feel like it is not deceiving people or being untrue to yourself; it is respecting yourself by having standards and treating others properly. As you get to know your colleagues, the time may come when for instance you want to tell them that you need to concentrate on your job rather than chatting in work time because you are autistic; you may feel that you know them well enough or it may be that you want to reassure them it's not that you don't like them. The most important rule is to listen to your gut instincts and to tell people when you are all calm, not blurt it out in an argument or while stressed. If your colleagues not knowing you are autistic is causing problems or misunderstandings and you feel confident that they will respond kindly and helpfully to your telling them, that is when you should start thinking about it; perhaps telling one or two people first rather than a whole team together.

Whether or not your colleagues know you are autistic, respecting boundaries and personal space is very important at work. Remember that people's boundaries are not the same with everyone they know; seeing someone else hug a colleague or ask them a personal question doesn't necessarily mean that colleague would appreciate you doing the same. They may have known the other person for a long time or they may be friends outside of work, or the person may have helped them with something which has created a bond between them.

It can be difficult to judge what is and isn't OK to talk about or join others talking about in the workplace. While you are getting to know the people you work with, it is best to let them show you what they are happy to talk to you about. Avoid asking questions about their lives outside of work unless they mention them to you. As time goes on, if you want to develop a more social relationship with a colleague you could try very general questions like asking what music they enjoy or what they like to do at the weekend, rather than asking about their families or where they live or go to outside work. The general questions can lead to more social conversation, whereas personal questions can feel intrusive even though you don't intend them that way. If a colleague mentions something personal to you then they will probably appreciate you taking an interest, for instance if someone tells you their child is in a school play or competition on a particular date. If they seem happy and relaxed when the time comes, wish them luck; if they are still happy and relaxed afterwards, ask how it went. Be aware of their mood though; if they seem quiet or sad or annoyed, it is best not to mention it as it may be that something went wrong and they don't want to talk about it.

Judging whether to join a conversation can also be difficult. If someone is talking very quietly or talking to their close colleagues about something personal such as a problem they are having or a family member being ill, do not try to join the conversation or stay to listen; even though your instinct is to want to reach out, the best thing you can do for them is to be discreet and give them space. If a conversation is about other colleagues, is an argument, or a debate about something that invokes strong feelings such as sport or politics or religion, that should also be left alone. If however a group of people you know and have talked with before are talking openly about something safe and neutral such as a TV show, that is a safer prospect. It can feel like a huge relief when people are talking about something we can relate to and think of things to say about, but be mindful of the impulsive responses that relief can cause; remember to try not to talk over people, interrupt or force the conversation onto a single topic for too long.

Developing social relationships

It may be that you would like to develop a friendship with a colleague but they prefer to keep their interaction with you just at work. This can be disappointing, but you must respect their wishes. It doesn't mean there is anything wrong with you or that they don't like you. Just as you have your own routines and comfort zones, so do other people and there are some people who prefer their lives to be set out that way, keeping most people in the context in which they meet them.

This principle applies not only to the people you see at work but also to people you get to know through email or telephone contact while doing your job. These relationships need to be handled extra carefully because they lack the clues and signals we get from having a person in the room with us. Even though it is true that autistic people often have difficulty picking up non-verbal cues when with other people, we do pick up some of them and we can also get clues from how we see those people interacting with others. Relationships which develop over the phone or through emails are more isolated and can be very deceptive. We can feel as though we have gotten to know someone well but not really know them at all; it is the familiarity of their limited but specific presence in our life that we have gotten used to and our creative imagining fills in the rest without us realising it.

Such relationships can develop very gradually over a long time so that before we even realise it, we are giving away more personal information than we ever thought we would at work, or we are shocked and hurt when the other person suddenly moves on or changes their behaviour towards us. These changes can happen because of something in their own lives or because they need to redefine the boundaries; often we will never know and this is very difficult for autistic people when we need clarity and consistency.

Sadly, there is a small minority of people out there even in responsible and caring roles who will pick up on others' vulnerabilities, sometimes before the people even know they have them, and manipulate situations to feel powerful or for personal or professional gain. As autistic people, we cannot afford to be too trusting of any apparent friendship which is based on work, especially where we have not developed it face to face with the person over time and have no mutual acquaintances to help us build a more accurate picture. It is fine to enjoy it but we must be wary and interact safely.

The incomplete knowledge of the other person in these relationships can draw us in with its mystery and excitement especially if our day to day lives are not going well and we feel unfulfilled; this can lead us into unwise choices and unsafe situations. When it is in a work setting, we are at increased risk of ending up in serious trouble. This would be likely to include having personal information we have shared read by other people as part of a disciplinary process. We tend to be very private people and even when there is no malicious intent on the part of the other person, by the time the signs of a friendship going wrong begin to dominate it can be very difficult for us to reach out to seek appropriate help before things get out of hand.

If any of this, work related or otherwise is familiar to you, even if you are pushing that uncomfortable realisation away and telling yourself that your situation is different, you need to step back and talk in confidence to someone you can trust. It is hard and it is exhausting and it hurts, but you must protect yourself from the potential combination of a painful loss and the worry of being in trouble plus your privacy being compromised.

This is not to say that all friendships which start out at work or through telephone or email contact are bad and dangerous! They just need to be looked at with extra caution and recognised for what they are. If they are genuine, they will either develop naturally as time goes on, or they will remain comfortably in place just as they are with no sense of needing to impress the other person or missing out on anything by it staying simply a friendly and enjoyable part of our job. Be open minded and wary of expecting too much when meeting someone for the first time and be prepared that one or the other of you may not want to meet again. Some people find it very difficult to tell the other person this and instead will avoid the subject. This again is difficult for autistic people; to stay safe, if it becomes something that is causing you stress, uncertainty or upset, back off and do not try to press the other person for answers. If contact tails off, let it.

Bullying in the workplace

If you feel as though you are being bullied, first ask yourself whether there may be another explanation; someone may just have a brusque manner or be doing their job in asking you to do something you don't enjoy, or their sense of humour may be the kind that is not obvious to you. Autistic people can get jokes and enjoy laughter, but don't always realise when others are joking and do not mean to be hurtful or offensive. If, however, something is happening that is making you feel bullied and you cannot talk to the person about it, do not try to cope with it on your own. Everyone has the right not to be bullied and to feel safe in their work. Talk to someone you trust who can help you to decide whether you are being bullied or whether there is another explanation you are not seeing because you are too close to the situation. If it becomes clear that you are being bullied, write down what happens, when and who else was there; keep it safe where nobody else can get hold of it. Talk to someone in an official supporting role; part of your support network or an organisation which can help. Stay true to your own standards of behaviour and engage with bullies as little as possible, keeping interaction to what is necessary at work.

In all aspects of your working life, remember you are doing a great job. You are showing courage, integrity and positivity just by doing the best you can every day, including the days when you just cannot manage; those days are a part of your enhanced battle and thus greater achievement.

Chapter 4: Getting into Trouble at Work

Disciplinary action was something I thought only happened to other people. I have always tended to be a people pleaser and a perfectionist. It sounds cliched, but it is the truth; I never thought it would happen to me, until it did. I know now that it isn't so simple as only either malicious people intentionally doing bad things or innocent people who have been framed or wrongly accused ever getting disciplined. Life is much more complicated.

There was a situation which built up gradually over several years involving a breakdown of a friendship with a work contact; there was fault on both sides. She behaved in an ambiguous way for a long time and eventually took a drastic course of action; I made unwise choices in how I dealt with the deterioration of a friendship I cherished. I tried to cope alone with emotional upheaval way beyond my capacity; I didn't know I was autistic, though I had medically recognised mental health issues. It was in fact the ongoing crisis caused by this darkest time in my life that led to my autism diagnosis. I had no idea about how autism heightened my emotions and felt so ashamed of my inability to cope that I didn't confide in anyone, either friends or medical professionals. I should have. I wasn't naïve but very unhappy and out of my depth. I gradually allowed personal feelings to get into work based correspondence and continued this after she stopped replying. It was common for her not to reply to every email; she was very busy, so I let myself think too rigidly instead of using common sense. I told myself that as long as she didn't tell me not to contact her (which she never did), I wasn't doing anything wrong; that it didn't matter because I wasn't contacting her all the time, perhaps on average once or twice a month, and I wasn't trying to contact her anywhere other than her workplace or approach her in person. I didn't know she was keeping my correspondence and had been since well before she stopped replying, though she didn't save her replies, until I was in serious trouble.

The suspension and investigation lasted three months and for a large part of that time I wasn't told the truth, though I suspected it from the day I was sent home. They told me it was a medical suspension arising from my team leader's concerns about my depression. They had to send me for a medical assessment to find out whether I could cope with a disciplinary and until that was done, they couldn't tell me the truth. I wasn't allowed to visit the office, contact anyone there other than my union rep and team leader, or go out of town without applying for leave. The ambiguity and uncertainty seemed to go on forever and in the meantime I had to pretend to my parents on our twice weekly phone calls that everything was normal. Later, I even had to eat with them on a visit the day before I was to receive the phone call which might be telling me I had been dismissed.

When my employers did tell me the truth, it was no surprise but it still devastated me. The two hearings were soul destroying. The boss was a decent, kind guy who before his promotion had worked with me in a supporting role for managing my stress. After the first hearing, he said he appreciated it couldn't have been easy for me. I told him, "It can't have been easy for you either, mate." I'm sure there were tears in his eyes. When I got to the second hearing, he indicated he had already poured glasses of water for the four of us present. Somehow I came out with "I'll get the next round"; he said "Oh, God love you!" I must do the responsible thing here and emphasise that I do not recommend calling the boss "mate" or joking at a disciplinary; it is not usually appropriate in that context and I was lucky it was taken well. I include this story to lighten a very grim page in a positive themed work and to show that humour and warmth can reach into the darkest corners.

I got a final written warning and went on to write this, my first coping strategies guide, to try and bring some good to others. As I was still undiagnosed, it was written with mental health as its focus but it is equally applicable to autism.

Getting into Trouble at Work

Immediate Action

When a crisis erupts, there are several steps which you can take to manage the situation and limit damage both practically and in terms of your wellbeing.

Practical

Involve your Trade Union if you are a member of one. Trade Union representatives are bound by confidentiality and are not there to judge you; they will have seen other cases like yours and will not be shocked, nor will they embarrass you by mentioning anything to you when back in the workplace. If you have any concerns and you work in an organisation with more than one branch, you may ask to deal with a union representative from another branch. As well as helping you to answer your case, your union may well have linked facilities for related help such as legal and financial advice.

If you are not in a union or wish to seek advice elsewhere, you can go to your local Citizens' Advice Bureau. If you are in a union, your employer may ask you not to take the issue outwith the organisation but it is unreasonable to deny you any access to representation and advice.

Tell your GP as soon as possible. It is very important that he or she is aware of what is happening and records it and the effect it has on you in your medical notes. This can help to ease and speed up the process of getting the help and support you need as well as giving you back-up for your case.

If financial hardship has been caused as a result of the crisis, seek advice and assistance as soon as possible. Although you may be feeling tired, overwhelmed, unsure of where to start and unwilling to tackle paperwork, it is important that you do so quickly as loans and benefits take time to be processed. Your union representative, Citizens' Advice bureau or benefits office will guide you through the necessary procedures.

Look up what other help may be available to you, for instance on the Internet at home or in your local library (try such keywords as "mental health", "employee rights", "counselling"). Support groups, mental health organisations and charitable organisations providing crisis support often produce leaflets (you may also find these at your GP's surgery) and websites with simple, clear advice on such aspects as your rights and ways to cope; they also offer links to other services. Looking them up will help you to feel more in control and less alone.

If you know why you are in trouble, prepare a statement before going to any meetings. Let your representative look at it beforehand so that they can tell you any amendments they think would be a good idea, or ask them to meet with you to help you compose it. Be factual, not emotional; at the same time be honest about your state of mind, health and anything which made things worse. It is important that when talking about mitigating factors, you still accept responsibility for your actions; if you made a mistake or did something wrong, say that you are giving explanation and context, not making excuses. List any attempts you have made to resolve the problem or to get help, such as approaching your GP and being put on a waiting list for counselling.

Wellbeing

Look after yourself. Resist the temptation to drink or use drugs; this will only make you feel worse and may lead to you making things more difficult for yourself. Eat properly, do breathing and relaxation exercises and try to maintain your usual sleeping pattern. Be careful what you say to colleagues or anyone else involved especially when your emotions are running high; avoid situations where you may end up doing or saying something you will regret and having to fear more repercussions. Where possible respect your employer's wishes but do not be afraid to ask questions.

Writing is very helpful; it can be an aid to slowing a racing mind, organising your thoughts and processing what has happened. Write down how you feel and how you remember what has happened; write letters to vent your feelings and then destroy them. This will help when you come to state your case; you will have vented those negative feelings which would be unhelpful and dangerous if they came out in the wrong place and also clarified the things you do need to say.

Focus on the present; do not try to look or plan too far ahead as you will get bogged down in "what if"s. Make sure that you have what you need and then concentrate on getting through each day. If plans you had such as holidays or courses are now in doubt, imagine yourself putting them away in a box in your cupboard or wardrobe and covering the box with colourful material; tell yourself that they will be safely kept there until such time as you can get them out again. Believe that whatever happens, you are going to get through this and the day will come to get them out again.

Do not suffer alone. If you are feeling unable to cope, go somewhere safe; a friend or relative's house or ask someone to come and sit with you. The Samaritans are always there to listen; you do not have to be suicidal to call them, they support anyone in distress.

If you are afraid you may harm yourself or anyone else, you must seek help urgently. Go to a friend or relative you trust, or to your support service, GP's surgery or hospital.

Aftermath

There are various techniques which you can use to cope as time goes on especially if you are away from work awaiting the next stages. There will be times when you find that you cannot stick to these techniques; allow for this but try not to leave it too long to get back to a coping routine.

Keep to any agreements made such as a schedule of contact with your employers.

Try to maintain your routine; eat and sleep properly, avoid turning night into day as this will make it harder than necessary to tackle the return to work. If you dislike daytime television and find you are staying up to watch programmes into the night, consider recording some and watching them when you are in during the day; at the same time do not become too reliant on television to fill your day. Local radio may be a better option as it will help you to feel more in touch with what is familiar.

Keep up regular contact with your GP and any other medical professional you are seeing. This allows them to support you and it is important that even if there is nothing they can do, your medical records are updated to log your state of health. Keep talking also to the people around you who support you; partner, friends, family, flatmates, colleagues (though you should maintain confidentiality and if you do not have a close friendship out of work anyway it is best to keep contact with colleagues casually social and avoid discussing work). Accept their offers of help and company.

Try to keep your sense of humour. This is very important for your wellbeing; it is as vital as eating and sleeping properly, though it is best to remain formal and practical in dealings with work.

If faced with possible unemployment, update your CV; you may not feel like doing this but it will make you see skills you have learned and experience gained, helping you to feel more optimistic and in control of your future. This will improve your self esteem and ability to cope with the crisis as well as boosting your awareness of your value as an employee. This in turn will help you state your case.

Use time off in practical ways; a good clearance in the home is highly recommended, though be wary of taking on too much at once and putting undue pressure on yourself. Tackle a room or cupboard at a time. This has a refreshing and revitalising effect and donating items to charity shops will make you feel good by helping others. Consider hobbies; art, languages, reading that novel you always wanted to but never had time. Get involved in the community; for instance check on an elderly neighbour, babysit, walk a sick friend's dog. Remember, though, not to make long term commitments which you will be unable or pressurised to keep when your circumstances change again. These are only suggestions; be occupied but do not go too far the other way and end up stressed.

Get plenty of fresh air and exercise. Go for walks, put on a CD and dance, go swimming. This is vital for your physical and mental health especially if not going to work means that you are not getting your usual quota of both. Exercise boosts the production of endorphins which improve your mood.

Keep concentrating on the present; avoid the trap of excess speculation about the future.

Maintain your self respect by treating others as you would wish to be treated; be polite and pleasant but at the same time do not try to be a saint. Allow yourself space and avoid added stress.

Accept that you will have to be self reliant; you may have to spend more time alone than usual and you will sometimes have to wait for people to be available. Prepare yourself for these times with relaxation techniques, materials for therapeutic writing, drawing etc.

Turning points

The time will come when you have to attend nervewracking meetings or be waiting for that crucial phone call. Have someone with you if you can but even if you have to wait for that call alone, there are ways in which you can cope with it.

You have the right to negotiate; ask to have meetings or receive telephone calls at a time when you can have a union representative or friend with you.

Write a list beforehand of things you want to say or ask.

When attending meetings, present yourself well; dress smartly and be punctual, be polite, show goodwill and thank the people involved for their time. If you are feeling overwrought before going out, release energy in a harmless way such as punching a pillow or exercising.

Make sure that your employer has informed you of your rights, such as the right to be accompanied, to ask for adjournments or to respond in writing; to have reasonable notice to return.

Do not drive to a meeting if you are likely to be distressed. If this means using unfamiliar routes and public transport, plan your route beforehand and however tempting it may be, do not drink alcohol even if not driving.

When feeling afraid, keep telling yourself this is short term and will soon be over; even if the news is bad, imagining it is usually worse than dealing with it in reality. It is amazing what we can cope with when we have to.

Distract yourself with a book, activity or music (though consider your neighbours and others in the household and keep the volume down if listening to music through the night). If you cannot sleep and feel the need to get out of the house, make sure you stay safe.

Back to work

Returning to work is bound to feel strange and daunting. This is a natural reaction for which your employers will be prepared. You can help yourself by making your own preparations.

If you will be getting up earlier again after a break in routine, especially in the dark mornings, adjust your getting up time in stages, arriving at your usual time a few days before the return. If you find it a problem getting up when you do not have a reason to, keep a reminder in bold letters where you will see it on waking, reinforcing that you are doing this to make it easier on yourself and that once you are up the day will soon start to get better.

Write out the things you missed about being at work; tea breaks with friends, enjoyable tasks etc.

Plan some simple, affordable and accessible treats; relaxing with scented candles, catching up with friends, taking a long hot bath. Unwind with something non-demanding especially on the first evening.

Tell your GP when you are returning to work and discuss any concerns.

Take all the support which is offered to you, both personal and professional; be honest about how you feel and any worries you have. Keep talking to your support network and do not bottle up feelings at the risk of them erupting at the wrong time and causing more problems.

Expect that settling back into routine will take time. Set yourself small, achievable goals so that you can frequently see and feel that you are making progress. If the memory of reward systems from childhood such as stars on a calendar is comforting, use them again in your own personal space.

Be prepared for questions; colleagues will be concerned and glad to see you back. If necessary have a cover story ready and agree this with your employers.

Be aware that there will be times when the reaction to what has happened will hit you unexpectedly. Plan how you can deal with this; a discreet breathing or relaxation exercise, a short walk around the room or a “timeout”.

Expect that for a time everything will feel strange; keep reassuring yourself that it will not last and you will soon be back in the routine again. A few familiar items around your workspace, within your workplace policy and health and safety parameters, will help.

Dress comfortably as much as possible; if you are limited in what you can wear, something comforting such as a scarf, cardigan or even slippers under your desk can help. If you have to wear a uniform, wear it at home for a few minutes in the days leading up to your return.

Be aware of your rights (for instance under equality law) but be diplomatic and raise any issues when you are feeling calm.

STAFF ENTRANCE
PAPER

Chapter 5: Redundancy

The only full time job I ever had ended in redundancy when our office closed. We were all gathered in the centre of the open plan workplace to be told; the blinds were drawn shut, which always seemed to me to be an unnecessarily melodramatic touch. The chief executive left her handbag unattended on the floor, which was either an oversight or a touching show of faith in the honesty of the Scottish people when she and her entourage had just told over 100 of us that our financial future was no longer secure. I remember the surreal sight of the burly security guard I gave the bag to, at that point not knowing whose it was, carrying it down the aisle. I'd love to say it was pink; that would be an even more amusing image, but it was black. There was a power cut across half the city later that afternoon. It was quite a dramatic, edge of a precipice sort of day even for those who weren't autistic. References were going to be an issue for me because of the disciplinary action I had on my record; I had one of the luckiest breaks of my life when a beautiful, compassionate and non-judgemental soul in HR received the email my union rep sent for advice and pledged to personally take on any request for a reference and give a favourable and balanced view, despite never having met me. I emailed to thank her; she replied concerned about how low I seemed given the way I was describing my lack of deserving her approach. I was so wary of email based friendship, it took a long time even once I had left employment, but Gabi persevered and is now one of my closest friends. She had been there the day we were told the news. We met years later on a sunny June evening in Edinburgh and reminisced about that stormy November day. She didn't remember the blinds being closed and she was away home before the power cut, but we sure laughed about the handbag.

I was glad to leave; if the office hadn't closed I wouldn't have lasted much longer as my fatigue worsened and my productivity dropped. I still treasure the fond memories I do have though. I despaired of the phones; their unpredictability, their urgency, the stress when I had to try to make out what people were saying when their mobile signal was breaking up and I was contending with background noise, but I did tell myself I was getting something of a classical music education from all the times I was put on hold. It was usually the Four Seasons or Greensleeves; I entertained myself listening out for the Brandenburg Concertos, Number 4 being the jackpot. I think I heard it once. Some of my colleagues already had me firmly consigned to the Uncool bucket and talking about anything classical probably didn't help my social standing, but I did have other colleagues who appreciated it. Perhaps the best memory of that kind is of the day one of the lads put his Smartcard in the computer upside down, which caused it to get stuck fast. As a succession of colleagues tried and failed to pull it free, I suggested we needed King Arthur. Whether the chap who eventually succeeded was pure in heart I have no idea, but the dramatic release of the card was certainly worthy of Excalibur coming out of the stone; in fact the sudden backspin sent a plant pot flying and smashed it to pieces. Working full time did give me some stories to tell.

Being made redundant is a huge change for an autistic person to cope with; it alters an entire routine, creates uncertainty and brings practical dilemmas at a vulnerable time. Even when in some ways it is welcome, as it was for me, it needs to be managed safely and constructively. I feel for anyone who is made redundant from a job they are enjoying and genuinely love. It is so important not to try to cope alone.

Redundancy

Preparing for the news: Psychologically

Dealing with rumours

There is always a lot of speculation when it becomes apparent that a firm may have to close or cut staff. What begins as guesswork with no root in actual plans or policy is repeated, exaggerated and ends up being passed around as fact; comparisons are made to other places and situations which may or may not be close to what the truth of the matter will eventually turn out to be. Although it is natural to talk through uncertainties, it is important to keep these unfounded and unconfirmed rumours in perspective. Remember that they cannot be taken as definite truths and try not to contribute to the process by keeping them going or adding anything to them. Even though you may make it clear that you are only guessing at what is to happen, it is quite possible that later on your and other colleagues' guesses will be repeated to others as confirmed facts.

Scare stories are unhelpful. You will hear them; you may well feel inundated with worst case scenarios. Step back from them; keep reminding yourself that your own story is unique and does not have to be dictated by anyone else's outcome, real or imagined. You may not be able to control every aspect of your own outcome but there is always some of it which is in your power to manage (see the following sections which focus on practical steps) and that is what will make the difference in the end.

Keeping a sense of proportion

This is very important for the sake of your health and for allowing yourself to be in the strongest possible position to cope; you need a balanced outlook, a clear head and the scope to combine preparing for the worst with a positive and ready attitude. Face the worst but seek the best.

Remember that worrying as it is, the prospect of your current job coming to an end does not have to be the disaster you may at first think it is. Your employment is only one aspect of your life and it is vital that this situation does not take over your thoughts to the extent that it harms the other good and constant things around you such as health, family, friendships and your own personal interests and leisure activities. Keep hold of the thought that your job is only part of your life and, although we need to have money coming in for other areas of life to continue to run smoothly, your current job is not the only possible source of earnings. No job is so unique that it cannot lead to another.

Looking after your health

Do not try to carry the burden alone. Talk to family and friends; do not add to the pressure on yourself by trying to keep the situation secret from the other adults in your household and anyone who will potentially be affected or can help you. It may be feasible and indeed wise to keep quiet whilst there are only unsubstantiated rumours but once you know that it is very likely you will have to deal with a change, it is best not to add secrecy to an already stressful situation. If your circumstances are such that you really cannot tell a partner or seek support from those close to you, then you must consider talking to someone in a professional capacity; your GP is a good place to start and your employers may have an employee support programme in place. Using these outlets is absolutely not weak; it shows strength of character in giving yourself the best chance.

Do not be tempted to seek refuge in alcohol, illegal substances or any kind of destructive or unlawful activity. There is nothing whatsoever to be gained from it and potentially a lot more to be lost; financially, socially, physically, emotionally and in terms of your own prospects just when you need them to be strongest.

Preparing for the news: Practically

General strategies

Write lists. It is an invaluable way of organising your thoughts and plans; what needs to be done, what you need to know, what you will need to take care of financially, who you will need to notify and so on. If you begin whilst you still have plenty of time, you can do a little at a time and still feel more in control if and when you receive definite news.

Take walks. As long as you observe safety and personal security precautions, it is an excellent habit to get into; it is free, healthy and gives you time and space to think clearly.

Employment related strategies

Consider visiting your local Jobcentre before you actually have to. It is bound to feel like a daunting step and emphasise the sense of strangeness if you go in for the first time when you are at the stage of having to look for a new job. Ask to take a look around and familiarise yourself with what facilities are available.

Update your CV. It will be helpful to have it immediately to hand.

Start making notes of examples from your day to day work; things you do well, problems you solve, ideas you have; times when you show initiative, help a colleague, "go the extra mile" for a client. These will be helpful in interviews when it can be difficult to think up examples on the spot; it will also help your confidence and belief in your chances of finding another good job.

Begin considering other possible jobs and careers in which you may be interested. Do not assume that you will only be able to do something which is similar to your current work. Look at your outside interests and hobbies; there may be opportunities there to build a new career even if they do not seem immediately obvious. Use your current job as a template; write down what you like and dislike, your strongest and weakest tasks. You can return later to any notes you make and ideas may come in the meantime as your brain will be processing them subconsciously.

Look into the possibility of courses or voluntary work. This does not necessarily have to involve a large time commitment; a couple of hours per week can be spent doing something which you enjoy and which improves your prospects in terms of skill and contact building. Even if it is difficult to be free at the same time every week to do something, for instance if you currently work shifts, there are options; volunteering hours may be varied, or you could do a correspondence course or learn a language.

Financial strategies

Prepare for a possible temporary cut in the money you have available. If you do this before you need to, it can be less stressful and also add to the reserves you will have when you need them. Look into cheaper options for meals, leisure activities and shopping whilst it may be done as an interest and even become a satisfying hobby. Do not commit to any unnecessary expenses and save up as much as possible.

When the news is confirmed

Continue with all the strategies you have been using when preparing for the news.

General strategies

Make sure that you have been informed of all your rights; that you have been given due notice and that you know where to go for all the help and advice you need. Guidance on getting financial, career and benefit advice will be available through your union, Human Resources department or local Citizens' Advice Bureau; most large scale employers when forced to make job cuts will provide access to training, time and resources to look for alternative employment and support through the process.

Look for inspiration from others who have been through the same upheaval and gained from it. At home or in your local library, use the Internet to search using such phrases as "Redundancy success stories" or "Redundancy changed life". Many people have been made redundant and found their way to a happy and fulfilling lifestyle which they wish they had discovered earlier.

Keep looking after your health. Exercise and eat properly; this will help your mood and make you better equipped to cope physically and mentally.

Take every bit of support which you are offered.

Employment related strategies

Stay loyal to your employers; show goodwill and work hard. You may not feel like it but it is the best thing you can do; it will recommend you well to future employers. Remember you will most likely need a reference from the employer you are leaving.

Consider your options very carefully if you have to make a choice, for instance between redeployment and a severance package. You do not have to take redeployment just because it seems the familiar and safe option; you need to consider whether it is likely you will only find yourself in the same situation again. At the same time do not go straight for a severance package because it means some time off and a lump sum. Take time to look at the good and bad things about each option and make a level-headed decision based upon which suggests the best long term future.

Financial strategies

Make sure that you know exactly what you will get in terms of severance pay and when it will be paid; take care not to overlook other things you may need to check on such as pension schemes and tax.

Get professional advice from a trained source.

After employment ends

General strategies

Try to maintain a daily routine; it is perfectly reasonable to make the most of your free time but do not leave it too long to get back into a lifestyle which will be compatible with starting a new job. Avoid turning night into day or becoming a "couch potato".

Take some time to rest and reflect if you can but do not lose the habit of staying active. If you slow down too much for too long it will be very difficult to pick up the pace again when you need to.

Set yourself other goals besides finding a new job; remember that work is only one aspect of your life and everything else which is important to you still needs your attention and energy.

Aim to achieve a balance between making your time in between jobs a positive experience and getting too comfortable with not having to go out to work. Keep reminding yourself of the good things about working and use every time you feel bored or cannot afford something as a boost to your incentive to get back to work.

Employment related strategies

Start applying for jobs before you really need to. It may take longer than you hope to secure another job and you can build up your jobseeking skills and techniques whilst under less pressure.

If you have been employed for a long time before the redundancy, accept that jobseeking now will not be the same as it was years ago. You will have to get used to different ways of applying and styles of interview; at the same time you are bringing a different set of advantages to the market as you now have a whole lot of work and life experience which you did not have before. See it as a brand new experience and an opportunity.

DO NOT GIVE UP HOPE.

Financial strategies

Do not blow your severance pay. Allow yourself some treats, a holiday or something for the home but make sure that you do not lose sight of the fact that this lump sum has replaced a regular income and will have to last, possibly for longer than you think.

Claim benefits as soon as you can; remember that as well as the money you need to live on, you need to consider less obvious issues such as maintaining your National Insurance contributions record.

Put into practice everything which you prepared during the stages of waiting for the news and leading up to this change in your circumstances.

Sources of information, guidance and support

Your Trade Union

They will provide general advice and support as well as helping you find more specific resources for your own particular needs.

Your GP

He or she is primarily responsible for any health care you need and is there to help if you are becoming distressed or unwell because of uncertainty. Human beings need security and structure; it is perfectly natural to find it very difficult to cope when changes happen which affect us but are outwith our control. Never be afraid or embarrassed to ask for help if you need it.

The Citizens' Advice Bureau

Here you can get general advice about all kinds of issues and speak in confidence to trained staff who will help you to work out where you need to go for more specific help.

The Internet

Although it is important not to take everything you read online literally and it is not a substitute for trained professional advice, you can find a lot of useful resources just by putting a few words into a search engine which relate to what you want to know. It is also a very useful tool for researching new career options and reading up about companies where you may wish to apply for jobs, or for finding career ideas related to your own interests and skills.

Your local library

Here you will find local information about what is on in your area; courses, support groups, leisure and social options for those on a budget as well as addresses of organisations which can help.

Your local JobCentre

As well as the obvious function of helping people to look for work, here you can access advice about the best way forward for you and also discuss in confidence any concerns you have about health matters, caring responsibilities etc. There are specialist advisers who deal with disabilities, including invisible conditions and they are duty bound to do so sensitively, discreetly, without judgement and in accordance with equality law. Whatever your concerns, dealing honestly with your advisers and being prepared to meet them halfway will give you the best possible chance of finding your way to a suitable and gainful new situation.

Telephone support

You can phone organisations such as The Samaritans if you are feeling overwhelmed and need to talk to someone. You do not have to be suicidal to call them and they will listen sympathetically to your feelings.

You can find out about organisations offering help and support in the telephone directory, online or in directories produced by some local councils.

There is a list of contact details including post and email options for a selection of organisations offering help and support, including The Samaritans, in the Sources of Further Help and Support section near the end of the book.

SUNRISE
VIEW

Chapter 6: Claiming Disability Benefits

This is one of the areas in which specialised autism support is most important. I have had long battles to fight in the past because although I had that support available, I was proud and stubborn and tried to do it on my own. Of course, that weakened my case as my pride stopped me from letting assessors see just how much I am affected. Once I let people do their jobs and help me, I gained not only much needed moral support and official backing but an increased awareness of my own profile of needs. However well we know ourselves, there are often things others can see that we cannot. We have never known any different so we don't realise how much extra effort something is taking, whereas someone trained to work closely with autistic people can pick up on signs we may be missing.

The diversity of the autistic spectrum is another reason why we should try to have proper professional backing when we need to claim anything. People assessing claims often do not realise just how wide a range of difficulties and levels of difficulty we have; they can also be influenced by popular stereotypes about autism. If an autistic person is able to make eye contact or doesn't talk exclusively about one special interest or speak in a monotone, it can confuse people. This is why we need to keep on talking about autism, its good and bad aspects and raising general awareness as well as making sure we are properly backed up and have informed representation when we need to reach out for the help and support we need.

However well prepared we are, with the stress and overload of an assessment we can forget to mention important points; it is most useful if we can have someone experienced with us to remind us when we should be mentioning something significant.

Keeping evidence for a benefit claim is a key part of putting forward a strong case but it is a distressing and demoralising thing to have to do. It is important to keep reminding ourselves of the things that go well and to keep those reminders separate from the upsetting details we are having to note down. Something as simple as making someone laugh or having a chat with a neighbour or being complimented on a nice smile can do a lot to counteract the bad feelings which writing about the negative experiences for a benefit claim can have. You may feel you already have enough writing to do, but try to find a minute or two to write a quick note of good moments like those; unlike the benefit evidence, keep looking at those positive memories as often as possible.

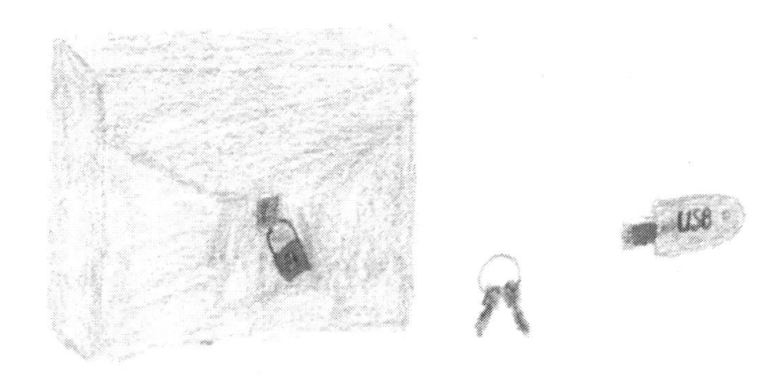

Claiming Disability Benefits

This chapter can be applied to Personal Independence Payment (PIP) or Employment and Support Allowance (ESA), or any benefits which replace them in the future. The advice applies to claiming for help with daily living and for those unable to manage full time paid employment.

Looking after your health and wellbeing

You are bound to be feeling nervous at the thought of claiming and especially of going for a medical assessment; this is perfectly natural and shows that your instinct to look after yourself is working as it should. It is a sign that you are already preparing to do what needs to be done, even if it does not feel that way. Look upon the apprehension, unpleasant as it feels, as meaning that you have already made that first step of beginning to deal with it.

Now it is time to start building on that first step and it is important that as well as planning how you are going to deal with the process itself, you take extra care of your general health and state of mind.

Do not try to cope with the anxiety and uncertainty on your own. It is vital that you talk to others whom you can trust about how you are feeling; friends and family will be better able to help you if they know what you are going through, even just by listening and making you feel that bit better for having gotten your worries out in the open. It is even more important that you talk to the people whose job it is to support you and back your claim officially; that is people such as your GP, counsellor, social worker or support worker. We will look in more detail at how they can help with your claim later; it is important that they know how you are coping so that they can help you to find ways to cope better and in the case of your doctor, consider whether you may need to take some medication or change your dosage for a while.

There are other things which you can do yourself and which will be good for your health generally as well as helping you to get through this period of uncertainty. Make sure that you are eating properly, sleeping well and getting plenty of fresh air and exercise; keeping to a routine will help you to keep your health and moods stable. It can also help to make it seem a less scary thought that one day in the future you may be able to move towards the possibility of working again if that applies to you. You do not have to be completely rigid about your routine; everyone, including employed people, needs a break sometimes! When you have a routine, the times when you do something special or different feel more exciting and fun. Just try to get up, have regular meals and go to bed at around the same time most days. If you drink alcohol (as long as there is no medical reason not to), it is very important that you do so in moderation and not for the wrong reasons. If you drink to get drunk, to feel better, to forget your worries, to fit in with company in order to avoid being alone, to help you get to sleep, out of habit or because you are bored, that is when it can become a problem and the longer you let that go on, the more hard work you are giving yourself to do in the future in order to cope and feel well, secure and calm. Any drugs which are not medicines prescribed by your doctor and in the dosages given to you are bad news, full stop; do not do it. You need a clear mind, physical and mental stamina and a positive attitude. It is not a disaster if you do not feel that you have all of those things all of the time; far from it. It shows that you do need the help and support which has led you to claim this benefit and that is all the more reason not to try to cope all on your own.

You might want to think about asking for your benefit decision to be sent somewhere other than to your home address, especially if you live alone; that will help to ease the tension of waiting for that official envelope to come through the door. You may want it to be sent to your support worker or to a friend or relative. Ask their permission first and you will have to make the request in writing to the benefits office to send it to a different address. Reinforce this request with a telephone call. Someone else can make the call for you but you may be asked to speak briefly to the benefits officer just to confirm that the person helping you has your permission to speak for you. If you do receive the letter at home, it is best that you do not open it when you are on your own; have a general plan for how you want to deal with it but bear in mind that with no way of knowing exactly when the letter will come, it is best not to be completely reliant upon any one person as it may come at a time when they are not immediately available.

Make sure that you do not let the worry of claiming or going for medical assessments take over and push everything else out of your mind. That will not help you and will only make it more difficult to face. Part of looking after yourself and giving yourself the best chance of a fair outcome is allowing yourself to get what enjoyment you can out of your daily life; keep your hobbies, your relationships and your sense of humour. Remember that this uncertain time will not last forever.

Making sure your needs will be fully described

Write down as much as you can in advance. This will help you to organise your thoughts and reduce the likelihood of forgetting to mention important things or being stuck for words on the day. It is much better to write things down as you think of them over a period of weeks or months rather than relying upon remembering everything on the spot during the comparatively short medical assessment. Be prepared for the fact that some of what you write down may well make you feel embarrassed or upset; it is a difficult and brave thing to do but the more examples you give, the stronger your claim is.

As well as writing general notes as you think of things, it is a good idea to keep a diary of day to day examples. You do not have to update it every single day, nor do you need to go into a lot of detail; a few sentences will usually be sufficient, though a few paragraph entries explaining more complex issues or events will also help. Some suggestions of what such entries may look like will be given later on but it is important to remember that the examples you give must be true to your own circumstances. It is relevant to say how you were feeling when something happened but it is best that you keep these descriptions short; writing too much detail is likely to make you more upset and result in an impractically large document.

Remember that you are not writing for anyone other than the people who need to read it for your claim; you are not writing as a therapeutic activity to vent your feelings, nor composing an essay, sitting a test of your writing skills or trying to interest a reader in the same way authors do when they are writing a story. You do not have to worry about spelling or about repeating yourself; indeed it can be useful to repeat yourself to make the point that a particular problem is an ongoing part of your daily life. The main rules you should bear in mind are to give the truth about your difficulties and to avoid swearing or saying anything which could be interpreted as threatening or offensive to benefits staff or anyone else. It is also advisable to stay away from making direct accusations such as "none of you believe me" or "you're all out to get me". The people reading your claim paperwork are not making character judgements about you; they have guidelines to follow and although it is understandable that it feels very personal to you when you are going through the process of claiming, they are not making their decisions based on forming any impression or opinion of you as a person and whether or not you "deserve" the benefit.

Keep your records or diary somewhere safe and private; if you are keeping them on a computer make sure that you back them up regularly and make them password protected if the computer is used by anyone else by whom you would not wish the document to be seen. It is a useful rule and safeguard to your health to decide firmly from the start that you will only have that document open for as long as it takes to write in it each time and that you will not read over everything you have written any more than is necessary (for example to check whether you mentioned something important or add something you just thought of for the appropriate date). Reading over it, especially as time goes on and the document grows larger, will only upset you unnecessarily, further reduce your confidence and self esteem and make you dwell on the negative things to the point where they begin to seem overwhelming and the positive things in your life lose their power to help you to get past the day to day glitches and setbacks.

It may be helpful if you can send your written evidence directly to the office dealing with your benefit claim before going to any assessments; if you know in advance when you are likely to receive a questionnaire, for instance when your claim is due to be reviewed, it is a good idea to start putting together evidence as far in advance as you can so that you can send it in at the first stage. Give copies to your GP and support workers; it will be useful for them to have the record of your difficulties and it will also help them to provide detailed and relevant statements to further strengthen your claim. They may also be able to see ways in which your condition has contributed to your difficulties which are not so obvious to you, as they are experienced professionals looking in from the outside and will have seen similar situations involving others with the same condition. Remember to keep a copy for yourself, securely put away where you know where to find it but will only see the contents if you specifically need to open it.

Making the examples relevant

If you are claiming ESA, remember that the focus is on why you are not well enough to work; if claiming PIP, the focus is on how your daily life is made more difficult including your leisure activities. When saying how often something happens, for instance feeling anxious using the bus, make it clear that it would happen more often if you had to go out more often and at times not of your choosing. An example might be to say "eight or nine out of ten bus journeys I make" rather than "a couple of times a week" if you only go out on one or two days; point out that it would be much worse if you had to travel in the rush hour or could not wait until you felt better after an anxiety attack before having to go out.

If you have worked in the past, try to remember ways in which your condition caused problems particular to the work environment which are eased, eliminated or less noticeable now that you are not working or not interacting with people to the same extent. Although mostly relevant to ESA claims, thinking about this could also help you to realise and remember examples which will help you state your case for PIP. This could perhaps include such things as:

- Fatigue and concentration issues
- Anxiety causing you to abruptly leave your post to seek a quiet space or to need to make frequent urgent trips to the toilet
- Being prone to intrusive thoughts and memories causing you to become upset, distracted or agitated
- Difficulty with social expectations and interaction with colleagues in the workplace
- Difficulty coping with customers and the public
- Problems coping with criticism even if it is constructive; feeling disproportionately upset by it or reacting in a defensive manner
- Problems adapting to changes in routine, tasks, priorities, equipment or procedures
- Difficulty coping with going to places you do not know well
- Misinterpreting communications by telephone, email or letter when there are fewer clues as to the other party's intentions, mood and expectations

- Misinterpreting face to face communications from people you do not know well because of lack of awareness of subtle clues such as body language and changes of tone
- Difficulty absorbing and processing instructions in a busy, noisy environment
- Difficulty working out your own role in following general instructions given to a department or group
- Difficulty in dealings with authority figures and navigating through the unwritten rules and "office politics" of the workplace
- Stress and pressure related issues
- Lack of sleep, disrupted sleep, nightmares, difficulty getting up and becoming alert at the start of your day
- Needing so much energy to cope with work that your quality of life and relationships outside work became affected or you turned to drink, did not eat properly, lost interests and hobbies or got no exercise
- Social withdrawal outside of work.

<u>Give specific examples</u> if you possibly can. If you faced disciplinary action for anything which arose as a result of your condition or in which you believe it was a contributing factor (even if you had not yet been diagnosed at the time), including warnings for sick leave or inefficiency, do not be afraid to include this information. It will be treated as sensitively and confidentially as the rest of your claim, as is your right and the aim of the assessment is to determine just how much your capacity to work healthily and gainfully is compromised by your condition, not to judge you all over again for having been deemed to have done wrong in the past.

If you are currently doing voluntary, therapeutic or permitted work, make it very clear that you are able to do this very specific job <u>only because it is of a type and in a sheltered environment suitable and tailored to your needs</u>, with a different range of rules, expectations and conditions from those in mainstream employment.

The quality of your life outside work if you were to be in a job is just as important a consideration as your suitability for employment itself. Everyone needs to be functioning well in order to be healthy and productive, in personal life as well as working and you have every right to have this taken into account.

How your examples should be recorded

You should make it clear at the start or end of the document that the examples are just a selection of the difficulties which you have encountered in your day to day life over the period of time for which you have been recording them; that you have picked out one or two things from each day but could not realistically write down everything every day as you are affected on an ongoing basis (all or most of the time) by all the factors which cause you difficulty and which would not affect someone without your condition in the same way.

There are two main types of example you should be recording; the ongoing symptoms (physical and psychological) of your condition and incidents which occur or are made more difficult because of the way your condition makes you experience life.

The symptom examples may include such issues as headaches, fatigue, bouts of more severe depression, anxiety or panic attacks, forgetfulness and sleep related problems including nightmares. They may also include an illness such as a cold which is not directly related but is made worse and more difficult to cope with by, for instance, your already existing fatigue or effects of your medication. Or you may be unable to take medication for something else because of what you are already taking. For ESA, remember that all of these things would be relevant in a work situation because they would make it more difficult for you to attend work, be on time and manage your tasks once there. When writing these examples, keep in mind whether you can say how they are caused or made worse by your condition; how they affect you more than they would someone without your condition. For instance if you have developed a headache because of worrying or becoming worked up about a minor event, say that this is why you had a headache and how long it lasted. You may mention worrying about your claim but keep it short; avoid overdoing it or criticising the people involved.

The incident examples are anything that has happened, in or out of your home, which had a bad effect on you even if they did not directly involve you; you could for instance have become anxious after seeing something happen amongst other people because it brought back memories or made you think about things which make you angry or frightened. When writing them down, consider what happened, how you felt and responded, whether your condition made it worse and in what way and how you were affected afterwards. You may for instance have had an argument with someone later on because of how you were feeling, or forgotten to do something important, cancelled plans because you no longer felt able to go through with them, become distressed or developed a headache. The incidents do not have to be dramatic. Remember that one of the most important things which you are putting across in your claim is that incidents which are quite commonplace and may well seem small and hardly even be noticed by someone without your condition are genuinely difficult and significant for you and can continue to affect you afterwards. You may also consider including comments by other people, such as a friend telling you that you are too sensitive; you don't need to put their name or give details about why they said it.

Try not to be too concerned about not having come out of an incident very well; the idea is to show that you are vulnerable in certain ways because of your condition and this includes making mistakes and not always coping very well with challenges. Nobody is going to look less favourably upon your claim because you snapped at someone or got upset or forgot to do something. It is important that you make allowances and do not let yourself become too disheartened when you are writing these things down. Always remember that you are having to do this because you have a health condition which is not your fault and does not mean you are less of a person; you need support because you have these difficulties and as a result of them, you have extra pressures to cope with. You are doing something very positive and courageous by seeking the help you need. If you are finding it too distressing collecting the examples, you must talk to someone you trust and keep your GP, support worker, adviser or whichever care professional you see regularly informed about how the process is affecting you.

What some examples could look like

(These ones are made up; remember that examples must be your own)

Symptoms

I did not sleep well and woke very tired. It took me 45 minutes to get up and I then sat on the couch for another half hour before making some coffee. I got washed and dressed bit by bit over the next two hours.

After misunderstanding a news item about possible changes to council housing, I became convinced that I would have to move and developed a severe headache which lasted all day due to the anxiety.

I woke several times through the night because of having a cough. As I was too groggy from the effects of the medication I take to help me sleep I could not manage to get up for a drink of water. I have therefore been overwhelmed by tiredness today and ate unhealthy leftover food because I could not face going to the shops.

I have felt very anxious generally and now have aching muscles in my neck from having been tense all day.

I lost concentration when preparing a meal and forgot how long it had been in the oven.

I became very upset after hearing a song on the radio which reminded me of a bad event in my life and kept on becoming tearful throughout the day.

I forgot to attend an appointment / take medication / pay a bill.

Incidents

Some teenagers were whispering and giggling in the bus queue. I became convinced that they were laughing at me. I glared at them and this made them laugh all the more. I became so angry I felt as though I could explode and the bus driver made a comment about the expression on my face which made me feel worse. I was so desperate to get back inside my house that I would not stop when a neighbour wanted to chat.

Someone bumped into me in the supermarket, giving me a fright, then tutted at me. I was so unsettled that I forgot to check the food I was buying for an ingredient I'm allergic to.

The phone rang just as I was about to go out to catch a bus. It was a wrong number. I was annoyed and told the caller to dial more carefully. I managed to catch the bus but as the call had rattled me I could not remember locking the front door. I also began to feel guilty for having snapped as the caller had sounded elderly. I could not concentrate on anything while out and almost walked out in front of a car. By the time I got home I felt physically sick and could not face eating.

I saw a fight outside a pub and it brought on a panic attack because I had once walked out of a pub just as a fight started and was picked on because I froze and so the people involved thought I was staring at them.

I had a big argument with a friend because she sent a joke text message which I took as a dig, not realising that it was just a forwarded joke. She said that she should have known better than to send it to me because I take everything so literally. That hurt me because I felt she was comparing me to all of her other friends, liked them better and intended to leave me out of everything from now on.

I misheard a shop assistant and handed over the wrong amount of money. He was impatient with me and there was a queue building up. I became so flustered I then almost walked out without my purchase. I will have to avoid that shop in future just as I already avoid another shop where a similar thing happened over a year ago.

At and after assessments

On the day

Make sure that you know your route well in advance and arrange to go with someone else if you can, ideally one of your support workers. It is useful to have someone there to give you encouragement, though you need to answer the questions in your own words. It will be useful if you can take a checklist to make sure you mention everything you need to and make notes when you need to remember what was said. It is courteous to the examiner to explain what you are doing but it is your right to make sure that the appointment is used in the best way; it is about getting the correct decision for you.

Dress comfortably; there is no need to wear a suit but avoid clothes with any words, logo or picture which could cause offence. Be on time and make sure that you have everything you were asked to take as well as any of your own notes which you have prepared.

Be polite and answer questions fully but do not feel that you have to make small talk. The medical examiner will realise that you may be nervous and it is important that you don't put up a front and hide your condition. You will probably be asked to describe a typical day; make sure you get to fully describe your problems and don't play them down.

Remember that the examiner will not know what the decision is likely to be, nor how long it will take. It is important that you do not add to your stress by reading too much into what they say or how long you are there.

Try to take some time to relax and do something you enjoy after the assessment; you may well feel tired, drained and unsettled by having had to talk about your difficulties in that setting.

Waiting for the decision

Keep on doing everything which has helped you to cope up to now; look after your health and keep on talking to your support network.

If you feel that something was not covered or that you forgot something, do not panic. Write down anything which you think of and talk to your support worker about whether it would be a good idea to send it to the office dealing with your claim or to keep it in reserve in case you should need it later.

Remember that even if you do not get the decision you want, you can appeal. Prepare yourself for the possibility and keep collecting examples if it helps; you may need to take a break from doing so if it has been upsetting you a lot but you may feel better for doing something practical just in case you do need to appeal.

A final note for those claiming ESA who feel they could work in the future with the right support

You may want to think about doing a bit of research just to take some of the fear out of the idea of eventually going back to work. You can do this without it committing you to anything and at this stage it is not something you would be advised to tell the people assessing your claim. Your support worker can help you to find out whether there are organisations which specialise in finding work for people with your specific condition and liaise with them to set up an informal meeting to chat about your circumstances and eventual goals. You may also consider looking on the Internet or in your local library for articles about people with your condition who have secured jobs in which they are happy and supported. Everyone's experience of any condition is unique so do not feel that you have to "live up to" these people; it is all about making you feel less afraid of the future. Remember that if and when you are ready to work, equality law is there to protect you and there are specially trained people such as Disability Employment Advisers and in-work support programmes to help people with your condition to find, keep and enjoy their jobs. You do not have to do it alone; the help is there for whenever the time is right.

Chapter 7: Moving House

There is a lot of belief involved in moving house; it is one of the most stressful things we do in life and we need to be able to believe we can do it and make the right decision about where to live. There has to be a balance between believing that it will all work out and doing the work we have to in order to give it the best chance of doing so.

I had been dreaming of a move to the Highlands for a quarter of a century before I finally did it. There were genuine reasons why it took so long but I have to admit I could have been up here sooner if I hadn't been so daunted by the scale of the task ahead. At the same time, I believe I moved here when I was meant to.

The first time I viewed a house in Aviemore, I came very close to getting it. I was the first to view and the prospective landlords both knew about autism from their work; they appreciated the positive traits which make many autistic people good tenants. There was a shared moment as we discussed our mutual love for Aviemore and at that point, the tenancy was mine. I knew they had other people to see and that I mustn't take anything for granted; it was a very long day waiting for the phone call. The weather was unspeakably bad that afternoon; low cloud and that kind of rain which seems just to be hanging there in suspended animation because everything is already saturated even the air. As I walked back to the place where I was staying, a very friendly ginger cat ran up to me and climbed up me as I bent over to say hello; a bright streak of colour through all the grey. I still have the blurred but distinctive photo I took on my phone of that sweet face reaching up to me. It was a comfort to me later that day when the lady rang and very apologetically told me they had decided to give the tenancy to someone else because they weren't sure I would cope if their plans changed in the next couple of years and they had to sell. I do believe they were genuinely sorry and that it was a difficult decision, but I would have appreciated them asking me how I would cope in that scenario rather than make assumptions. I knew it wasn't realistic to expect to get the first place I went for. It was still a shattering disappointment and I felt as though that cat had been sent to me to give me hope that my dream was still there, just not quite within sight yet. It was only a few weeks later that I saw the second place I went for; bigger, more central and slightly lower rent. My honesty and openness impressed the landlord. I travelled up on Leap Year Day 2012 to view the house; on the first of March I signed the lease. I had made it happen.

Three years later in Albion House I told the story of that ginger cat to Jeni who had recently started working there and I showed her the photo on my phone. "That's Chucky!", she exclaimed; she had been fostering him at the time. It just blew me away to realise that the cat who ran to me and gave me warmth and a morale boost on what became such a dark day was living with someone who would eventually be my friend and colleague at the autism service I was dreaming of being involved with. I arrived just in time to help with setting it up. I am very happy in my lovely home and although I know the day will eventually come when I have to move on, I will remember that balance of faith and proactivity.

Moving House

The first steps

Getting started

It is a good idea to have a folder with plastic pockets and subject dividers in which you will keep papers to do with your move; lists, notes, receipts, contracts, letters. This will give you a focal point as well as helping you to break down the big effort of organising a move, turning it into a series of smaller and more manageable tasks. Use the dividers and pockets to group the contents into categories so that you can find things easily, for example everything to do with utility companies, benefits, medical matters. You may find it helpful to write To Do lists on different coloured paper according to priority; it will help you to get everything done when it needs to be and as time goes on you can always transfer items from one list to another. Checking your lists on a regular basis, top priority first and remembering to cross each task off as you complete it will help you to feel in control and to boost your confidence by seeing how much progress you are making.

Getting ready

There are several preparations you can make even if you do not yet know when you will be moving. First of all, plan how you are going to make the process as easy on yourself as possible. It is well known that moving house is one of the most stressful things we do in life; when you have health related issues which make it even more difficult, you really need to take care of yourself.

Make sure that the people around you know that you are going to be extra busy and need more support, whether by being there to talk to, giving you practical help or allocating more time to meet with you in their working role. Keep your support network, both family / friends and care professionals, informed of your plans and how you are getting on; ask for tips and experiences from people who have been through the process of moving if it is something you have not done before.

Get accustomed to the techniques you are going to use to help you through this busy time. Practice your time management; make lists of your daily tasks, even those you know well just so that you get used to working from notes. Develop a habit of doing things within a certain time and include enjoyable activities as well as chores to make it more comfortable and familiar, such as reading a magazine or taking a walk within a set time. If you have children, including them in these strategies will help the whole family to cope more effectively as well as making them feel like an important part of the team and making the hard work more fun.

If you or a member of your household has particular dietary requirements, it is important to think in advance how you are going to manage this when you are not in a position to follow your usual catering routines because of things being packed away or allowing for the likelihood of there being days when you have too many demands on your time and energy to be able to do what you usually would. Find out whether local restaurants and takeaways can accommodate any specific needs, both in your current area and where you are moving to; consider what foods you can have available which will keep and which can be provided quickly and simply. Family, friends and neighbours may be able to help by storing foodstuffs for you and providing a space to prepare and eat them.

Expect and acknowledge that you will be under a lot of pressure for a while and feel a stronger reaction than usual to other day to day stressful situations. Decide in advance how you are going to deal with this and what techniques you can rely upon; breathing and relaxation exercises, time-outs, helpful thoughts and a firm awareness of your priorities; to save your energy for what is important, getting yourself through the big move and looking forward to the positive result of settling into your new home.

Planning your move

Making preparations

Start to save up if you can. In addition to the actual cost of the removal, there will be a lot of associated expenses such as redirection of mail, administration fees for some change of address procedures such as certain insurance policies, extra telephone calls and postage, meals when your kitchen is all packed or you cannot manage to cook, taxis or extra petrol for going to viewings and getting rid of items you have cleared out. It is important to have some extra money available to help you to organise your move in safety and comfort.

Decluttering your home

A very good way to start the physical process of organising a move is to have a thorough clearance in your current home. This will mean there is less for you to have to pack, unpack and find places for as well as getting you into the way of working towards the big move; you can use it to get familiar with the time management and list making techniques you will need. List room by room all the cupboards, drawers, units and spaces you need to clear out; they will vary in size and complexity so you can set yourself guidelines as to how long each is likely to take and fit them in around your other activities. Try to do something every day. Recycling and taking unwanted items to charity shops will give you a boost as well as making the task ahead feel less daunting. At the same time, get used to your relaxation techniques; they will then be easy to follow during the actual move.

Planning whatever you can in advance

You can start at any time to make lists of the people and organisations you will need to inform of your change of address. As well as going through your address book and correspondence, check your bookmarked websites on your computer as this is likely to remind you of some more organisations. A list of suggestions to get you started is included further on.

Start to work out what packing materials you will need. Some firms offer packages of moving boxes which say they are for a particular size of house, usually by number of bedrooms but it is wise to take this as a very rough guide and expect to need more. Measure the drawers, shelves and cupboards you will have to empty and allow extra space for protective materials; you will need bubble wrap for your breakable items and you can also use clothing and towels as padding. It is better to have more boxes than you need rather than find yourself short.

Prepare your folder with the pages on which you will write your To Do lists once you have a date for moving. The most urgent tasks include giving notice where you live now, arranging redirection of your mail, informing benefits offices (it is best to write and back it up with a telephone call if possible and remember benefits mail does not get redirected), booking your removal firm (you will need time to compare quotes and secure a booking for the right date), letting your support network know and making sure you have plenty of medication to last you up to and beyond the move. Then you will need to gather your packing materials, arrange to get any furniture you are not taking cleared out, informing other companies of your upcoming move and organising the transfer of services such as your phone, Internet and gas / electricity. If you are moving to another local authority area, you will need to make a new claim for Housing Benefit and Council Tax Reduction if applicable to you; this will take a few weeks to process so start it early. In the lead up to your move, you can then be free to focus on packing so that you do not have too much to do at once; it is very tiring. Then you will have a final To Do list for when you have moved; registering with your new doctor and dentist, cancelling direct debits you no longer need once your accounts are settled (for instance if you change energy supplier at your new address) and updating your details on the Electoral Register, to get you started.

Looking for a new home

As you look for a place to live, keep a notebook and pen with you whenever you are out and about so you can write things down as they occur to you. They can then be transferred into your folder as you review it. Tasks for your To Do lists will keep on occurring to you; you won't think of them all at once so get into the habit of making notes when you can.

If you are moving to a new area, familiarise yourself with what it's like to live day to day life there. Subscribe to the local paper; see if it has a local radio station you can listen to online. These are valuable sources of information as well as making the transition easier.

You will need to know about local transport, shopping and where to find such amenities as the doctors, dentists, Citizens' Advice Bureau, library, branches of your bank, schools and vets if applicable. You can get a copy of the local telephone directory once you move; local newspapers sometimes have sections with useful numbers such as the local police station, which is reassuring to have a note of. Your support workers can help you to find out what is available in your new area; it is important not to presume it will be the same as where you are now and you should also ask them about the possibility of arranging some transitional support for you while you get used to a new set of surroundings.

Viewing a new home

If you are going to meet strangers and view a property, it is vital that you look after your safety. Any reputable website or agency will have guidance on this. If possible do not go alone; make sure someone knows where you are going, who you are meeting and when you expect to be back. Try to keep appointment times to when it will be daylight; it is perfectly reasonable to ask to see an unfamiliar place during daylight hours. Make sure you have a taxi arranged in advance if necessary; do not accept lifts and always have your mobile phone with you, charged and switched on.

Measure the rooms both in your own home and the places you are viewing. It is very difficult to visualise how the room sizes compare, especially with and without furniture.

Be willing to ask questions at viewings and take notes. Finding out about your responsibilities in terms of insurance, bills and Council Tax liability as well as things like where the fuse box is and where to turn off the water, electricity or gas, which companies supply them and what method of metering and payment is in place will save you trouble later on as well as impressing a prospective landlord with your sense of responsibility, improving your chances if they are interviewing several prospective tenants. If you can, find out if there is an active phone line. Look out for things you may need in the new house which you did not in your current one, such as gardening tools or parking permits; pay attention to what features are different about the new home. Be honest, friendly, polite and positive but do not disclose any personal details if you feel unsafe doing so; if your instincts are telling you that you may be taken advantage of, listen to those instincts and trust them. Do not carry around or part with large amounts of cash; get everything in writing and have it checked over if necessary before you commit to leaving your current home.

Making the move work for you

Once you have found a new home and signed the paperwork, it is time to put all of your preparations into practice. This is the busiest time; the move will dominate everything but remember to take care of your health and to allow yourself time to look forward, adjust to the changes and enjoy the journey. Now is the time to make sure your medication is well up to date and keep your doctors and support workers informed about how you are coping; be open to all available help and input from others.

Start thinking about what clothes you want to keep aside for the week or so before and after moving; allow for any unseasonal weather and choose what you can mix and match so that you can have enough to last you and still feel comfortable. Remember that whatever you wear will inevitably get dusty and creased from time to time. Plan your meals for the last few days before and first few days after the move and make sure there is extra credit in your phone.

As you pack, label each box as soon as you seal it up with which room it is for. You do not have to be absolutely strict about all the contents being for that room but bear in mind which room it will be most convenient for you to be unpacking it in. Keep one box for "last in and first out" items such as your kettle, set of cutlery and crockery for each member of the household, toiletries, soap, tea towel, hand towels and a toilet roll, washing up liquid, phone charger, snacks, rubbish bag and medicines; clearly label that box for opening first. If you do not wish to take calls on your mobile phone, your land line phone will go in this box too as you will want to keep it connected for as long as possible in case the removers need to contact you. As you pack, be aware that your familiar home will start to look and sound different; sounds will have a slight echo and by the time you are well through the packing, it will no longer seem like the home you know. This can be very disorientating and tiring but it is helpful to look at it in terms of easing the transition; you are not suddenly leaving it the way you always knew it. Your new home will have seemed similarly bare and had an echo; that will disappear as you come to the exciting part of making it your own.

On the day of the move, have a light but nourishing breakfast; you will be feeling very tense and you will need to keep your energy levels up. Keep your lists to hand so that you will not have to worry about missing any of those final day tasks such as reading the meter, turning the electricity off and leaving the keys with whoever you need to. You are bound to feel strange as you leave your home for the last time; say goodbye in your own time and then focus on looking forward to your new home.

Settling in

Be prepared to be tired for several weeks or even months; you have achieved something enormous in moving house and you should feel good about that and go easy on yourself. It takes time to recover your strength especially when you are getting used to a new set of surroundings.

The administration involved in changing your address will keep on generating more small and irritating tasks for a while when it is the last thing you feel like after all your hard work. This is an inevitable part of modern life. Reminders will cross in the post with information you have sent; you may be asked questions you have already answered. Keep on using those relaxation techniques; take a deep breath, remind yourself that the hard work is done and take one day at a time.

Get to know your new neighbourhood at your own pace; you will take a few wrong turns and need time to get used to routes to and from places in daylight and after dark. The feeling of unfamiliarity will not last long. You will need a bit of faith to believe that after all you have done but you really will get there. Keep a close watch on pets until they are settled; keep cats indoors for the first few days as they may try to return to the old address. Getting to know people is something to do at your own pace too; you can give a friendly smile and say hello without having to tell anyone your business. It is your move and your life; make it special, make it work for you and enjoy it as much as you can.

Appendix: Some people you will have to tell about your move

This is not a definitive list; you may have others and some of these may not apply to you.

Doctor
Dentist
Hospital and any other medical care or support provider
Benefits (it is best to notify each one individually; include your National Insurance number and tell them both by letter and telephone)
Employers, union and work contacts
Schools and colleges currently attended by any of your household
Your personal contacts; family and friends
Electoral Register
TV Licensing
DVLA and any other organisations to do with your car
Bank, building society and credit card or loan companies
Vet
Company responsible for details on your pets' ID microchips
Clubs and societies to which you belong
Newsletters, newspapers and magazines to which you subscribe
Charities you support
Online sites such as home shopping, eBay, Amazon and PayPal
Insurance providers
Utility companies (electricity, gas, telephone)
Internet service providers if you dial up from a land line
Shop loyalty cards
Catalogues
The local councils involved for Council Tax, whether or not you claim any discount on this and whether or not you are moving to a different area.

Chapter 8: Having Work or Repairs Done in Your Home

This is something we all have to deal with even when we are not the person in charge of running the household. We need our homes to be the predictable safe place we return to when the world is exhausting and chaotic, even in a good way; coming home after an exciting day out or a relaxing holiday is still important and enjoyable. When we have to let someone in to do work which means moving things around and disrupting our routine, it is a big thing to cope with. We can come home to get away from, or at least get a bit of space from, all other distractions and stressful variations to our routine but when work has to be done in our homes it can feel as though there is nowhere to relax.

I am very fortunate in that I have an understanding, kind and accepting landlord and lady who live close by. They know I am autistic and do everything they can to make sure any necessary work is done in a way which involves me in arrangements and at the same time minimises my stress. They achieve this by not being afraid to ask me questions about how to make things easier and by making all the tenancy paperwork precise and clear as well as always keeping me informed, well in advance and in a friendly way. I chose not to include them in the acknowledgements to this book because, like me, in a small town they like to keep their business private. I am forever thankful that I found their advertisement for a tenant and made the best move of my life.

I was reminded of the need for this chapter, written after the rest of the book was finished and on the point of going to the next stage of publication, when it happened to arise that I would need to give access to an electrician for a routine safety test. It brought back memories of a year earlier when my main storage heater broke down and the person who came to fix it couldn't find my house; the street I live on has quite a few clusters of houses leading off it which are all part of the same road. The poor guy made the genuine mistake of not realising there was more to my text than showed on his screen and didn't scroll down to see the part where I asked that my mobile number only be used for texts, not calls. I was unprepared both for giving directions and for the three calls he made to my mobile, the last of which was from so close by I looked outside for inspiration on how to make myself clearer and saw his van. I was in an advanced state of stress by the time he got to my house and I let him know about it! I learned from that to be better prepared.

So did my friends and neighbours whose house and cats I looked after while they were on holiday many months later. The husband had arranged for the ceilings to be painted while they were away as a surprise for his wife but didn't get the chance to tell me. I went over to let the cats out in the sunshine to find a van in the driveway and the front door wide open; how we laughed when my friends got home about what might have happened to their unsuspecting decorator if I had gotten hold of a baseball bat or a frying pan! I am not serious about the violence of course, but the discovery certainly added an unexpected twist to my quality time with the fabulous Mitzi and Matilda.

Mitzi and Matilda. Shown here with kind permission from their people.

Having Work or Repairs Done in Your Home

It is always stressful having to let people you don't know into your home to carry out work or repairs, but sometimes it is necessary to make sure your home is safe and comfortable for you to live in. Getting important equipment such as your boiler or gas heating checked regularly not only can prevent it breaking down and needing a much more disruptive repair, but may be a legal requirement. Household equipment will break or need replacing from time to time. It is lovely having your own space but if you live alone, this is balanced by the fact you will occasionally have to cope with letting people into your house to check or repair things.

The most important thing you can do to help you cope with this situation is to prepare as much as possible in advance. If you own your house, you will need to know what equipment you have to get inspected and how often in order to comply with the law; if you have a landlord or are in social housing, it is their responsibility and they are obliged to tell you before sending anyone. You can expect to be given the chance to arrange an appointment for a time that is convenient for you, but you may have to have inspections or work done by a certain date. Make sure you keep all paperwork about your tenancy, insurance and anything in your house which needs servicing together in a safe place and look at it every so often; write on your calendar when you will need to arrange work.

If you are arranging work yourself, make sure that you find a reputable tradesperson with the appropriate qualifications and safety certificate. Someone you trust may be able to recommend a person or company; if you have an individual landlord or rent from a private agency, you should ask them if they have a preferred contact and keep them informed of any work you are planning to have done. Your utility provider (for instance gas or electricity company) for the relevant equipment may be able to advise you on what qualifications and safety certificates you need to make sure any tradesperson has.

Once it has been decided who is doing the work, find out as much as you can about what to expect. As well as knowing the date and time of day, you might want to ask:

- What is going to be done?
- How many people will be coming?
- Will they need to visit more than once?
- How long is the work likely to take? (Be prepared for the possibility this may not be knowable in advance)
- Will you need to do anything before or after their visit, such as moving things out of the way of where they will need to work?
- Do you need to be there while they are working?

Depending on your individual needs, you may also want to ask:

- Is the work going to be noisy?
- Will they be using anything with a strong smell?
- Will things look different or need redecorating in your home after the work is finished?

In most cases a good tradesperson will clear up any dust or mess after doing their work but you may still need to spend a bit of time getting your home back just the way you are used to it.

You might find it easier to get someone you trust to be at your house with you or to be there on your behalf while you go somewhere else. Your landlord might want to be there anyway when work is being done; if not, check with them that you are allowed to ask someone else to be there in place of you. Your support network can help you to approach your landlord about this if you are distressed by the prospect of having to be there. If you are having work done while you are away, make sure you let neighbours or anyone who will be keeping watch or looking after your house know that people will be coming in to do work, so that they know nothing wrong is happening.

You or whoever is in to receive tradespeople must make sure that they are who they say they are. Make sure you know the name of the person or company and check identification, which all genuine workers will have and be happy to show you. Do not be pressured into agreeing to any work which is more than what you were told would be done. Never arrange or even discuss work with any stranger who comes to your door unexpectedly saying they have seen something needing repair; these people may not be genuine and anything they show you may be fake. If you have a landlord, including social housing providers such as the council, it is they who must authorise all work; if you are the homeowner, ask for quotes and reasons in writing and time to consider any suggested additional work then get advice from someone else before deciding if it is needed and offered at the best price. If a worker takes offence at you not agreeing to extra work, you have the right to ask them to leave; tell your landlord if you feel unsafe.

If you have particular requirements to make communication less stressful for you, such as asking for no calls to your mobile phone, make these clear to the workers and to your landlord. You do not need to go into details about why. The work may be necessary and as such not of your choosing, but you are still in charge of your own home life and entitled to reasonable boundaries. The work is being done for you; you are important.

There are a few practical things you can do to make the process smoother and less stressful for you. If you have to clear out cupboards or drawers before the work starts, take photographs of where everything is before you start moving it; this will help you to return it to the way it was. Move anything breakable or important to you (as is sometimes called "with sentimental value") well away from where the work will take place. Think about what someone who isn't familiar with your house might need to be told; for instance if you have a cat you keep indoors, they will need to know to be careful not to let it out.

You might also think about how you would direct someone to your house. Telling someone how to get to your house can seem very different to the familiar journey you are used to making; having to think under pressure to respond to a phone call from someone who is lost can be very stressful. Many people now have access to devices or phone apps which give directions but these do not always cover the fine details of residential areas. Think how you would direct someone from a central landmark such as a church, railway station or local business which they should be able to find, then prepare detailed directions with landmarks, road names, where to turn and in which direction as well as where not to turn and describe what to look for to recognise your house. Remember someone who doesn't know the area as you do won't recognise places by the way you are used to thinking of them; they need landmarks they will definitely be able to see. For instance, "The house with the two Siamese cats" won't help unless the cats are conveniently sitting there when the person you are directing drives past! An example would be something like "Turn left off the High Street into Church Road; look for the church on your right. Keep going past the next two roads leading off on the right; there's a bus stop on the left hand side of the road and my street is the left turn just after that. My house is on the right hand side with a rowan tree in the garden and a blue front door; you will see the house number on my bins next to the door." It would be useful for you to have these directions written down or saved in your computer to use again in future; you could add a photograph of the outside of your house. Remember to update the directions if anything changes, such as a shop having its name changed or your door being painted a different colour.

Always remember that anyone doing work in your home is obliged to treat you, the house and your belongings with care and respect. They should ask permission before using anything of yours, including electricity to do anything which is not part of the work such as charging a phone, and they should not enter any room they do not need to. They should also ask before turning on a radio or any music even if it is on their own devices which do not need to be plugged in; they should accept it without question if you say no or ask them to turn it down. It is reasonable to allow them to use your toilet, though they should still ask you first; many tradespeople work long hours with few breaks. If you are uncomfortable with them using your hand towel, have a guest towel out ready before they arrive. Close the door to any rooms, especially bedrooms, they will not need to go into.

If you wish to offer them refreshments, keep in mind that some larger companies do not allow their workers to accept food or drink in a customer's home; it may also be that they have already had refreshments on earlier jobs. So if they say no, it doesn't mean you have made a mistake; you cannot know what their bosses tell them or what they have had to eat and drink before coming to your house. You do not have to offer any refreshments; there is no set rule but some people like to.

Many people who make a living doing work in other people's homes are used to making a lot of small talk. While it is far too much of a generalisation to say that no autistic person is ever comfortable with small talk, a lot of us do struggle with it especially in stressful situations and it can feel very intrusive. They may make jokes, talk about things you don't find interesting or ask you questions about things like your hobbies if there is evidence of those in view such as cross stitch pictures or sports magazines. Remember that to them, it is a way of being friendly and nice; they cannot necessarily see or predict your discomfort. You are not obliged to have a conversation which is more than what is relevant to the work, but you should be polite, for your own sake as well as theirs. "I'd rather not talk about that, I don't know you well enough" is more likely to make the visit end well than "That's none of your business". If they ask inappropriate questions, for instance about whether you have a partner, or if they show too much interest in your valuables or anything that makes you feel uncomfortable, this is outside the acceptable limits of small talk. You should take notice of your instincts if you feel uncomfortable and talk to someone trustworthy in confidence about whether you should complain. If you don't want to have to deal with small talk, have something prepared that you can be getting on with and tell them you would rather leave them to their work and get on with what you are busy doing.

It is very rare for damage to be done by a good tradesperson but if anything does go wrong, take photographs with a device that records the date and time. If an insurance claim is needed, leave the damage as untouched as possible without leaving anything unsafe and contact your insurance company as soon as you can.

If it feels right to disclose your autism and this leads to a very positive experience, consider making their details available as a recommendation for other autistic people by telling any autism related groups or services you are involved with. This is an important aspect of autistic community and sharing good examples to be learned from.

Chapter 9: Travelling

Everyone in my life and quite a few passers by know how I feel about the Highland Chieftain; that train is the golden thread running through my life and has been for over 25 years. I love train travel in general. It can still be a stressful experience though; delays, noise, uncertainty and interaction with people can all be concentrated on a journey. I have had some spectacular delayed journeys in my time, though I have also made some friends. Barbara and Jean both came into my life on disrupted December journeys on the Chieftain when they were already travelling in difficult circumstances; despite the different kinds of adversity we were all facing, I was able to help them and they in turn took the time and effort to make me aware of skills I hadn't realised I had. Sometimes we are so busy being perfectionists and thinking about everything we wish we had said or feel we should have done better or quicker, we miss what we have actually done and the difference it has made. It is a blessing when people then reach out despite their own pain and tell us.

The part in this chapter about locking train toilet doors was brought to my attention by a TV advert for a well known Scottish soft drink, wherein someone is caught out by the door not being locked properly; it was an amusing and timely reminder of a situation I know does happen from stories I have been told by friends who work on the railway. The advert is very funny, but something like that happening in real life would be particularly unsettling and difficult for an autistic person to recover from, hence giving it a special mention in my travel tips. The most colourful story I can tell from personal experience involved a classic moment of comic timing as I walked through the carriages on the Highland Chieftain one fine summer evening, passing a toilet just as a lady called out an instruction to her friend inside which sounded very strange out of context! I realised later that she was talking about the manual lock which had to be turned clockwise and the actual lock was out of alignment with the arrows beside it, so that it needed to be turned right up to the hour position rather than the quarter to position as the arrows indicated. What the lady said to her friend through the closed door just as I happened to walk by was "I think you have to shove it right up". I wish I could have seen the look on my own face. This was in First Class too! Travelling on my own in fits of laughter, it was a good job the train wasn't busy.

In all places, not just toilet doors, I do prefer a good old solid manual lock that you physically turn. I despair of anything that has to be swiped or electronically read; don't even get me started on the ticket barriers. I know they are there for a reason but I dread the embarrassment of my ticket being rejected. It is a good idea to keep anything which has a chip or magnetic strip separate from mobile phones as there is some evidence that they can still interfere with the stored data, though improving technology is gradually eradicating this problem which used to be more widespread.

Travelling

Planning your trip

When booking seats, it may help if you can see where in the bus, train carriage or plane you will be sitting and how many other seats are next to or opposite you. This will help you to prepare yourself. Many companies will have a seating plan they can show you.

If you can choose when to travel, be aware of times when a lot of people will be travelling to and from nights out as it could get very crowded and noisy; you should also check for any big events such as concerts or sports fixtures which will make your route particularly busy.

You should make sure you have a plan for what to do if anything goes wrong; keep a fully charged mobile phone with plenty of credit and contact details stored for someone who can support you by call or text. Have enough to entertain and distract yourself if there is a delay, such as a book or game and some comforting objects which you can hold discreetly if you do not want to draw attention. Consider carrying an autism alert card in case you become too stressed to express yourself properly. Find out where the local tourist information office is.

Look up as much as you can about your journey; make sure you will recognise the uniform of people who work for the transport company so that you know who to go to if you need help. Look on websites or ask to see plans or photographs of stations and terminals you will be using, especially for making connections; allow plenty of time to catch connecting services, know where they are leaving from and find out what the company's policies are if you miss your connection. If you have a concession card, be ready to show it if you are caught in any delays as the transport company will have a duty of care to help you. If you are flying, make sure you know the rules about luggage; how much and what you may not take, even within the UK.

If you are going somewhere you have never been, especially another country, make sure you do some research about local customs and traditions. Non-verbal gestures can mean different things in different countries, including sexual or insulting meanings so do not use them unless you are sure. Some countries expect people to dress a certain way in public or not to do certain things outside or on particular dates, especially religious festivals, and in places of worship. Read articles by people who have been to those countries; look up articles online by searching for phrases like “customs” or “visiting” and the country to which you are travelling. You will also need to know whether you need any vaccinations or whether there is any health related advice such as drinking bottled water. Make sure you are covered by a good travel insurance policy. Know what currency you will be using, how to get more if you need it and the contact details for the British consulate if you should need help. Be very careful if drinking alcohol as measures can be larger and stronger than you think or are used to, or affect you more quickly in a different climate.

When booking accommodation, check whether you will be able to get access to it any time you need. Some establishments, especially bed and breakfasts run from people’s family homes, expect that guests will be out all day. You may become tired or overloaded more quickly than usual in an unfamiliar place and need to get into your room to rest, take refuge or make a telephone call in a quiet environment.

Consider your needs when choosing what type of accommodation to go for. A small, friendly guest house may sound more appealing than a big hotel but you are likely to find people making conversation and asking you questions as you eat your meals. Hotels are less personal if you want to be left alone, but they can be quite complex in their layout and take a bit of finding your way to and from your room. If you are going somewhere for more than a few days, self catering may be an even better option; you will be able to keep to more aspects of your own routines, diet and so on. Especially in cities, there is an increase in availability of self catering lets for less than a week at a time, though very rarely for single nights.

Before you travel, talk to your support network about any worries you have and let them help you come up with the best ways of dealing with them. This will help you to concentrate on looking forward to your journey and setting out in a strong, positive frame of mind.

During your journey

You do not have to talk to strangers (apart from necessary interaction with transport staff), but try to avoid coming across as rude to people if they do attempt to start a conversation. Judging tone of voice especially when stressed can be difficult for autistic people and it is easy to sound brusque when we do not mean to. You don't have to explain yourself; just calmly and politely say that you don't like talking when you're travelling. If someone persists after you have asked them to leave you alone, they are doing wrong and you have every right to ask staff to intervene; the same applies if someone is occupying your reserved seat. Of course the reverse applies too; if you do like chatting to people but someone tells you that they want to be left alone, you must respect that. Wearing headphones, even if not actually listening to music on them, is a good way of keeping your distance. If you do listen to music, though, make sure that you stay aware of what is going on around you so that you do not miss important announcements or instructions.

When waiting to get on a bus or train or for a flight to be called, make sure that you do not go out of range of hearing any announcements even when you have all the details you need; occasionally, something such as the platform from which a train is due to leave may have to be changed at short notice.

If there is a delay, this is bound to be stressful for everyone and especially for you as an autistic person. Remind yourself of all the details you have looked up in advance such as how to recognise the transport company staff; remember that other people will be stressed too even if they appear to be coping well. You cannot know how other people are feeling or what their circumstances are. Tell the staff if you have a connection to catch; they will be able to advise you whether the connecting service is able to wait or what other arrangements can be made. If the delay is going to cause other problems relating to your health such as needing to eat certain food at certain times or if you need a quiet place to go to phone your support network, have this written down so that you can show it to the staff if you do not want to talk about it in front of other passengers.

On any delayed journey, you may have no choice but to endure a difficult, tiring and uncomfortable wait for a while; keep controlling your breathing and your thoughts, concentrate on being safe and getting through each moment. Look after your needs as best you can, but remember you are part of something bigger; being polite and considerate to others will give you a huge sense of achievement and is part of taking responsibility for your own wellbeing. Recognise and respect your limits; if you are becoming ill or unable to cope, seek help from transport staff and let them know you are autistic. You can provide them with the details of your own support contacts who will guide them on how to help you. Do not try to cope by engaging in unsafe behaviour such as getting drunk; this will only make you vulnerable and cut you off from a lot of the help that would otherwise be available to you.

It is worth mentioning to take extra care with locking toilet doors especially on trains. Some newer trains have toilets with an open / close button and a separate lock button which only works if you wait a short while after the door closes; often the lock button (which may just have a picture of a key or a padlock) will start to flash a few seconds after the door closes and the lock will only work if you press it then. People occasionally get caught out because they press the button too early and think the door is locked when it isn't. There should be instructions beside the buttons which tell you exactly what to look for and how you will know the door is locked. There is usually no separate unlock button; the open / close button both unlocks and opens the door.

Pay close attention to your personal safety and the security of your belongings. Do not leave your valuables unattended, particularly at or just before a station when on board a train. If travelling late at night or at any quiet time, be wary of anyone coming to sit unnecessarily close to you; try to sit near families or the driver. At the same time do not sit too near to others, especially families with children, in a carriage with lots of empty seats; they do not know you and may not realise that you are sitting near them to feel safe, so they may feel uncomfortable.

While you are away

When you are in an unfamiliar town or city, make sure you know where you need to go and how to get a taxi you will know is genuine if you need one. Do not carry too much cash with you and be careful how much you have to drink; your responses may not be the same as they would in your familiar surroundings as you may be so busy processing additional and new information, you could be more tired than you realise or lose track of when you last ate.

If you get into conversation with locals, it can be interesting and a lot of fun but there are some things you as a visitor need to be wary of. Locals may talk about their town in a way which sounds as though they are criticising it or complaining about living there; sometimes they are. However, they may not appreciate a stranger who is not from there joining in. It is best just to listen; not to contradict them but not to add any criticisms of your own. It is also advisable not to get too involved with conversations about locally emotive issues such as sporting rivalries. Do not be afraid to say honestly that as an outsider you don't want to risk saying the wrong thing. A safer way to contribute to the conversation is to ask questions; where they recommend for a meal, do they get many tourists, is there a local paper or radio station. If you ask questions, listen to the answers!

It may be tempting to try to impress people with your knowledge of the town but be very selective. If it has one famous product or resident, they will get asked about it a lot. If you have read or heard something positive connected with the town, that should be a safe topic but if it involves something such as a tragedy, a crime or an event having gone wrong, it's best not to mention it.

With a creative autistic imagination, jokes, puns and plays on words about the town or anything to do with it may seem momentarily tempting, whether you think of something yourself or remember something you saw or heard. It can be easy, especially when drinking, to be so caught up in the rush of thinking up something witty and topical that you only see the skill with words and forget to think about the implications. However pleased you are with a clever thought or timely memory, do not risk causing offence; keep it as a thought. Such an ill-judged remark could cause a good, happy time which should become a treasured memory to turn sour in an instant; it could be at best distressing and confidence damaging, at worst endangering.

Use similar caution when visiting local businesses such as specialised cafes or themed attractions if there is more than one similar business in the town. The two (or more) businesses may be rivals, so even though it seems like a relevant topic, it is best not to talk or ask about the other similar ventures. If you want to decide which ones to visit, ask at your accommodation, or look them up on review sites before you travel.

Be aware that local people might use slang terms, nicknames or old names for local places and other expressions which have stayed in use out of habit; people sometimes use these terms forgetting or not realising that visitors will not understand them. They will usually explain if you remind them you are not from there and don't know what they mean. Unfortunately, there are some people who will take advantage once they realise someone is unsure in their company. If you start to feel uneasy or unsafe, trust your instincts; calmly and politely say you have to go and then leave. Do not tell them you are autistic or say anything to confirm your vulnerability to them.

If you need to ask for directions, try to find a trustworthy source such as a uniformed official or go into a shop, restaurant, café or other open, family friendly business. Most people you meet will help if they can, but there are a few people who find it funny to send someone the wrong way. This is rare, but one drawback of being autistic is that it can be difficult to read others' responses and motives. Taking photographs on your phone at turning points can help until you get used to a new route, but be aware of what you photograph (more on this later in the chapter).

You should be prepared for possible unexpected emotions and reactions while you are away from your familiar surroundings, even when you are on holiday somewhere you really want to be and are enjoying your time. Overload can hit unexpectedly, as can homesickness for your own surroundings or the services on which you rely. It can take the form of sudden worries about things at home or imagining bad things happening. This can be distressing especially when you don't know what has triggered the feelings. Acknowledge them for what they are; a response to being away and doing different things, just as your body can experience discomfort after the treat of a rich meal even though you enjoyed every mouthful. Think of these unexpected and unwanted feelings as a kind of emotional indigestion; if they do happen, don't be afraid of them or feel guilty for having them. They are a part of your autistic intensity and they will settle. If you find them taking over, lasting a long time, stopping you from doing things you have planned or making you too upset, try to distract yourself with a good book, interesting activity or TV show. If you are still struggling, contact someone who knows you well and understands your autism.

Be very careful when taking photographs or filming. Although you see it as capturing souvenirs of your trip, it is very important not to do anything which other people may object to or misunderstand. You should not film or take photographs of children you do not know, or child orientated places such as schools and playgrounds. Although it is fine to take photographs in some busy areas where children are present, such as a city square or tourist attraction, some people misuse images of children and many parents and carers are very wary of strangers capturing children on film. The people who misuse these images do not always use what they have taken themselves; many of them look on the Internet and copy other people's pictures and footage without permission. You should not take any images of private property including gardens and vehicles without asking permission and taking images of pets may also be misinterpreted as intent to steal. Ask permission before taking photographs of people where they are the main subject or filming them doing anything. Do not use flash photography in stations, near roads or anywhere else where the flash may be a dangerous distraction. Some places, including tourist attractions such as museums or art galleries, do not allow photography or filming so look to see if there are any notices up or if it is mentioned on any brochures, leaflets or tickets. Taking images of anything related to security anywhere, or of transport in some foreign countries, can get you into a lot of trouble. If in doubt, ask staff and respect all instructions.

DIARY
MY
HOLIDAY
MEMORIES

Additional advice: Travelling abroad

As I have mentioned in the introduction, I have never travelled abroad. Faith Wilson who has worked for many years with NHS Highland and carries out autism diagnosis has written an excellent guide to safety when going on holiday which covers many of the issues involved in travel abroad as well as points relevant to the UK or both.

Faith has very kindly given permission for me to include her article so that the travel advice in this guide has a wider scope. All the following travel advice is in her words.

Holiday / Travel Advice

E111 - Keep a note of the card number in a separate safe place, in case the card goes missing. You will need this if you require medical or dental treatment, present it to staff when you arrive at the hospital and before treatment starts if you are able to. This is only valid for European Union countries.

Passport - Make two photocopies of the photo page, leave one at home with someone you know well and trust, take the other copy with you and keep it somewhere safe. It is wise to fill out details on the back for emergency contact.

Insurance documents – Make two copies, leave one copy in the UK with someone who knows you. Take a note of the emergency contact number and carry with you at all times.

Flight tickets - Keep a separate note of your flight details, including your flight number, in case they go missing. Most airlines have electronic records of pre-booked passengers but may ask for some evidence of booking.

Currency - Keep receipts of transactions. Store your cash in a hotel safe or locked in your suitcase. Only take the amount you will need out and about with you.

Luggage – Follow the rules about packing, being careful not to pack any prohibited items, airline details will provide detailed information. If someone asks you to carry any items for them, check that the contents are not illegal. If your luggage goes missing or becomes damaged, you will have to complete a form before you leave the airport. You should go to your airline desk to request a form, or ask one of the airport staff.

Medical - If injured or unwell it's important to use only the recognised public hospitals. There are many privately run medical clinics abroad and some are eager to get customers. They may try to entice you in for treatment only to produce an expensive bill when you go to leave. Your insurance company will not pay this fee. When you arrive at the resort it is a good idea to check where the nearest hospital is and to get the phone number to carry with you.

Prescriptions – Make sure you have enough prescribed medication or treatments to last your entire trip and allow a bit extra for the event of delayed flights. Check that the country that you are visiting will allow the medication that is prescribed or obtain proof from your GP that it is essential that you take same.

Alcohol - Measured units may not exist, many bar tenders pour free handed from the bottle. Watch out for drink spiking and avoid leaving your glass unattended. Cocktails may be cheap but are also very potent, it is easy to get very drunk without realising. Strong shots of local alcohol may be offered free of charge with a meal. Try to count how much alcohol you are drinking and stay within safe limits. Alcohol poisoning is not pleasant. Be aware that some ice cubes can cause stomach irritation too.

Dehydration - High temperatures mean we lose a lot of body fluid and essential salts through sweat. It is important to keep this balance stable to prevent illness. Remember to drink water regularly (alcohol of any form does not count as hydrating fluids and does more damage). You can get sachets which contain the salts that we need to remain healthy, dissolve in bottled water to drink.

Water – check that your destination has safe drinking water. If not, use bottled water with the seal intact. Avoid ice in cold drinks, and be careful of salad produce which may have been rinsed in tap water.

Heat and sun - Avoid falling asleep in the sun, sunburn is painful, prickly heat can be unbearable, and heatstroke makes people feel very ill. The hottest time of the day is from 12-2pm, it is best to cover up during these times or to find some shade. Use protective cream or oil and remember to apply regularly. Wearing a light hat is a good idea in very hot countries. If skin becomes red apply aftersun or aloe vera.

Safe sex – It is wise to use protection in the form of condoms to prevent disease or unwanted pregnancy.

Emergency money - There are pre-paid money cards available that can be handy as an emergency back up. They are similar to a credit card in that they have the Visa Electron symbol and the microchip, but there is no credit, you fill the card with cash via a paypoint prior to travelling or as a savings system. They can be used exactly like a credit card to pay, up to the amount you have put in prior to travelling. Various companies offer this service, but it is worth comparing as each company has different terms and conditions.

Security - Keep a hold of your rail tickets as some railway stations are automated now and you would need them to place into the machine to exit. When travelling, be aware of using your phone, ipad, ipod or any other expensive equipment in an obvious way, some people may see it as a commodity worth stealing. Be discreet if possible.

Faith Wilson.

DEPARTURES
TRAVEL
SAFETY
TIPS
PASSPORT

Springtime rainbow over Druimuachdar Pass on the Highland Main Line

On the "Highland Chieftain" train to Inverness in summer

Autumn sunset over the Kessock Bridge, Inverness

Aviemore Station, winter

Chapter 10: Appointments and Meetings

My own involvement in some of the participation type meetings referred to in the second part of this chapter has been an interesting journey. It still is. I feel that my learning curve in this aspect of autistic life is more like an event horizon. Much of the advice I can offer comes from observing and talking with much more successful autistic participants and our experienced colleagues. I have gained some knowledge and strategies; that when joining a cause or taking up an issue in a new area, the most important thing to do at first is research and listen. Proactivity and keenness ought to be established by asking questions and listening to the answers before introducing ideas and suggestions when joining an ongoing project where there is a long history of local politics.

I arrived uninvited on the Highland autism scene when my move up here was still in the planning stages; I failed to give due deference to the fact I was not yet a local and I was soon put in my place. I tried too hard to make up for my disastrous debut at the early meetings and impress some very high up, charismatic people, only succeeding in making more faux pas which still make me cringe to this day. My continuing participation became much more behind the scenes than I originally intended. This was partly because of the bad first impression I made on the key people but perhaps even more down to the effect it all had on my confidence and self esteem. I found it very difficult to be around the various groups and committees because I could no longer sustain the mask of coping and being permanently positive. When I first met people up here, I could do it because although I was very keen to impress, it was less personal. As time went on after I moved here, people were no longer strangers; they were around my life but not in it, just there enough for me to feel the absence of the friendship I should have been in a position to be cultivating with them as my colleagues were. These key people were invariably gracious and friendly towards me when they did see me, but there were barriers there which greatly saddened me. There had seemed to have been a bond of sorts established after the earliest meetings which my colleagues in Edinburgh anticipated I would build on but that only began to happen after a lot of perseverance. Building trust and talking with experienced colleagues; really listening to what they said even when it was hard for me to believe, eventually led to better times.

I have written all of these guides to try to offer hope and a chance for others to benefit from my experience and learn from where I have gone wrong. This in itself is a way forward. I like to believe that it is very rare for a situation to be completely unsalvageable; I am only now, as I finalise this book in early 2016, beginning to put my first disastrous attempts at formal participation behind me. I am happily and constructively forming working relationships with others who are becoming more involved with autism issues. There is also, I am very happy to say, an ongoing renewal of cherished early friendship. This has only been made possible by courage, honesty, time and goodwill on both sides. In the meantime, I learned that knowing when to step back and take time to regroup is a skill in itself. Perseverance and tenacity are valuable strengths but even more so when they are balanced by using discretion.

Appointments and Meetings

Whether we are attending one to one appointments or bigger group meetings and conferences, it can be a very daunting prospect. We are out of our routine and often dealing with an environment which is not autism friendly. We are attending because we want to get something out of it; to solve an issue, get some help or a chance to put our ideas and opinions across. There are ways in which we can make the most of these chances and reduce our stress.

I have used the word "meeting" throughout this section for simplicity; the advice can also be applied to appointments and conferences.

Preparing

Write down important things you need to say or ask, highlight the most urgent ones and remember to keep looking at your notes to make sure you have said everything you want to. Plan to tick things off as you say them; you could draw a box beside each item to remind you to do this. Don't be afraid to ask for time to make notes as things are said in the meeting which you will want to refer to later.

Make sure you know the route to where you are going for your meeting. If it is nearby, you might find it useful to travel the route beforehand as a practice and to make it more familiar on the day. Check if there are going to be any roadworks, engineering works or anything which could make your journey take longer; your local paper or news website should have some information. On the day, you will still need to allow plenty of time in case any unplanned delays happen; make sure you know who you will contact and how if you cannot get there on time. People will understand that these things do happen, and being able to let someone know will help to reduce the stress of any delays.

Make any needs you have known in advance; your support professionals can help you with this. This includes any needs related to your autism and any other health issues or disabilities you have. You may want to check whether there is somewhere you will be able to go in the building if you need a break, or find out if your meeting can be scheduled for a time when the building is quiet. You also have every right to ask for a meeting to be rescheduled to allow someone to go with you if you need support. Remember you are entitled to all reasonable adjustments to make sure you get what you need out of your meeting.

When planning the day of your meeting, be prepared that you are likely to be tired afterwards; do not put pressure on yourself by scheduling anything demanding or energetic for the rest of that day. If you are working, it may be a reasonable adjustment for you not to have to go back to work that day after the meeting if it is going to be a difficult one for you. This is something you would need to organise with your employer.

At the meeting

If you feel in awe of other people there or of their position of authority, you may have heard some people jokingly advise imagining those individuals in an undignified situation, often involving the bathroom or wearing fewer clothes than they are. This can help to make them seem more human and less scary, but as autistic people we can be prone to inappropriate or nervous laughter and a funny imagining might distract us. It might be safer to think of them doing something which is simply very ordinary, like doing their shopping in the supermarket, cleaning the house, gardening or putting out their bin. The important thing is to remember, by whichever thought works best for you, that they are people just the same as you and no more or less important.

If you find anything difficult on the day such as the lighting, temperature or noise in the room, do not be afraid to say. Non-autistic people may not even notice something which is bothering you; other autistic people may not be affected by the same things. It is important that you tell someone and give them the chance to help. It is easy to think that a noise or smell which feels overpowering to you must surely be noticed by others but our sensory perception is so unique to each of us, it may not even register with them. If something is causing you difficulty and it is not possible to do anything about it, then that added difficulty must be allowed for by everyone present, including you. Give yourself the time, and the credit, you deserve.

Ask all the questions you need to. Write down any which occur to you during the meeting when it is not your turn to speak; this will save you from building your stress levels trying to remember as you wait. If time is limited or you don't get the chance, keep a note of what you still need to ask and make sure you have the correct, up to date contact details to put your questions afterwards. Let the relevant people know that you still have some questions; it may be possible for them to meet with you and anyone who is with you for support after the main meeting so that you can ask your questions in a less pressured environment. If there is not time on the day, agree a deadline for a response.

Participation events

As an autistic person, you may get the opportunity to go to events where people in responsible roles are looking for feedback, ideas and opinions from autistic or any disabled people. These events are often about planning services; what is or should be available to help disabled people and their carers to get the support they need in all parts of life. This may be things like health, housing, education, transport or employment. It is very important that autistic people get to go to these public meetings and be heard, however we communicate. At the same time, the meetings can be very hard work as they are about issues which make people feel very emotional and not everyone will agree. People sometimes end up having arguments or the discussion will move very quickly and it can be hard to cope with the intense energy and overstimulation in the room.

All of the advice in the rest of this chapter about preparation for meetings and looking after your needs also applies to participation events.

There may be an interaction badge or similar system in place for a bigger event. If there is, you should be told about it in the papers or instructions you receive when you book your place. Even if you do not intend to use an interaction badge, make sure you know what they look like and what they mean, so that you can do the right thing by those who are wearing them.

However strong other people at the event may seem, remember that you do not know how they are really feeling or what they have been through. Everyone has their ways of coping and people - including you - may well appear more confident than they are feeling. This also applies to the people who are in charge or representing authorities and service providers. It may be that several of the people there know each other and it could feel as though you are trying to join in with an established group. Remember that this does not make you any less welcome or your input any less relevant. People naturally go to speak to people they know and appear to interact more easily with them because they already know things they have in common; professionals may not have seen their colleagues for a while as they are all on busy schedules. If you don't want to join in with the social conversations before and after the formal business and during breaks, you do not have to. People should understand that you need to save your energy for what you came to do; participate in the event itself. Quiet spaces should always be made available at larger events for autistic people; if the event relates to disability in general, you may need to arrange this in advance as a reasonable adjustment.

Never feel that your participation is less valid or impactful because you need to take part in a different way: having an advocate there with you; listening and learning on the day, processing and responding afterwards in your own time; communicating with choice cards or pictures. The very fact that you need to do things differently, as do other autistic people, is the whole point of why these events need to happen. If you are not fully enabled to join in the way you need to, then that is a problem for the organisers of the event to be concerned about, learn from and do things differently in the future. They need to know about these difficulties so that they can help you and others.

You may feel that there are things going on which are not being clearly explained or talked about openly, especially if you are attending a participation event for the first time or in a new area. This can be a very real, disheartening barrier for people who have had the courage to go to an event after a lifetime of feeling this way about the world around us. The important thing to remember is that you are there to do something positive and deserve to feel comfortable. There are often good reasons why people are careful what they say; there may be confidentiality issues, or they may not want people who are not involved to overhear, or they may not be sure how other people will react when they do not know them. Local organisations may want the same outcomes but they do not always agree about how to get them; there can be long running disagreements which are very hard to resolve. Many autistic people pick up on tense atmospheres very easily and it adds pressure when we then worry about saying the wrong thing because we don't know the full story. It is best to keep focused on your own ideas and experiences which you have brought to the event; if you are sharing a personal experience, avoid mentioning the names of people or organisations involved when you are in a group where people might know anyone you mention. Concentrate on looking for solutions; what should happen and any ideas you have which might make things better.

There should be agreements and instructions regarding confidentiality but protect yourself anyway. If you are telling a story which involves another person, do not identify them without asking them beforehand. If you want your own experiences to be treated as confidential, say so; this will make it clear to other people. Think carefully about whether you want to share anything really private or sensitive even if it is relevant; you can ask to give information more privately to a specific person if you would rather not talk about it in a group.

Keep in mind that other people there may have difficulty with turn taking or knowing what is a reasonable amount of time to keep talking. It can appear that they are dominating the group but it may well be a part of their autism; they may also be speaking for the first time about something which has been causing them problems for a very long time and releasing a lot of frustration from years of feeling unheard and helpless. It is the responsibility of those leading the event and any groups or workshops within it to manage this and make sure that everyone gets time and space to join in as they require. Facilitators do make mistakes; like anyone else, they sometimes don't quite get it right or get done everything they need to. If you feel you missed your chance, don't take the responsibility upon yourself; use the feedback options which should be made available at the end of the event, or make contact afterwards when you have rested and feel calm. Talk to your support network about what you feel went right or wrong at the event for you; their perspective will be very helpful as you decide what you have learned and how you want to move forward.

If you are putting forward ideas or suggestions, be prepared for unexpected reactions. It is good practice to share ideas with someone you know and trust before taking them to a group, especially a big event where you don't even know all of the people there. Others' knowledge, experience and perspective can be very different from yours and what seems like a very good idea to you may not work for them; they may express this in ways you find harsh.

Remember that one of the drawbacks we face as autistic people is we sometimes think very specifically and do not see things which others can. We also try too hard at times because we have so much empathy and want so badly to make a difference or to find the acceptance and approval we have craved all our lives. With all of this in the way, our ideas can sometimes have flaws and pitfalls we cannot see, especially when we are excited and enthusiastic. We think creatively and we think pragmatically but sometimes the two do not quite come together. Or we can have an idea which is very good in itself but it is not the right time.

We become focused on our idea; we work on it, treasure it and fine tune it to the best of our own perspective and ability. It can be very shocking and hurtful to us when we do not get the reaction we expect, or when others go straight to telling us about a flaw even if it is minor. We then face further pain, embarrassment and frustration when people do not understand the intensity of our disappointment and reactions. We may never be able to see or take comfort from any discussion which starts from our idea and goes on to adapt its good points, never knowing that we did make a difference because the end result looks so different.

We all need to protect ourselves from the effect these setbacks and rejections have on us. We cannot protect ourselves from them happening, but we can find ways of coping better when they do. You are not alone. Just as with ideas and suggestions you might make at work, you need to focus on the effort and courage you showed which nothing can take away from you. Remind yourself that it is all a part of the daily success you achieve by living with the difficult side of autism and still continuing to reach out for the greater good.

The Story Of
CHANGE

In 2015, the Highland Autism Strategy Group was formed to continue with the work formerly done by the Highland Autism Improvement Group (called HAIG). This work is to make sure that services for autistic people, their families and carers meet the standards set by the Scottish Government's Autism Strategy.

The Highland Autism Strategy is being written to achieve the same thing in this area, bringing in more detailed local knowledge of what life is like in the Highlands. This includes making sure that people in rural areas far from the bigger towns do not miss out.

It needed to be made clearer what is being done and who is responsible. To help with this and find more ways for autistic people to be involved at all stages, two new levels were defined. The Highland Autism Strategy Group is a small committee of professionals whose job it is to answer to autistic people and carers. The more extended Highland Autism Network Group is made up of autistic people, carers and people who work with them. This wider group is involved with discussions, ideas, sharing what is going well and what needs to be better. Its role is consulting autistic people, their families and those who work with them and guiding the Strategy Group.

In November 2015, at a meeting of the working group who plan open events to do with the Highland Autism Strategy, people spoke of some confusion with the names. The new wider group was being referred to as "the Network group" and other such names which are similar to existing organisations. There had been a reluctance to use its full title because these groups often end up with an acronym (a name made from their initials) and HANG was obviously unsuitable!

It was discussed that the Highland Autism Network Group is as much a name for what is being done as for a group of people. What is being done needs ongoing consultation and engagement; always asking and involving the right people - autistic people, their families and support networks - about what they need and how best to get it right.

At that point, an autistic member of the group realised that if we surround that network group with consultation and engagement, the unfortunate acronym HANG becomes the much more positive and appropriate CHANGE. There was an instant celebration! Then we got on with it.

Consultation **Highland Autism Network Group** *Engagement.*

That's a lot of words; just look for CHANGE!

This is an example of what can happen when determination (or stubbornness!), learning from experience and persevering are combined with the right environment.

I am the autistic person mentioned who created the CHANGE brand and designed the logo with the speech bubble. My work with the event planning group is a joy.

Story of CHANGE reproduced here with kind permission from Arlene Johnstone, Chair of the event planning group.

Chapter 11: Feelings and Emotions

As well as coping with our own amplified emotions, we have to deal with the feelings of others and this can be so difficult as we try to read them through the clamour of our own minds. So often our problem is not too little empathy but too much; we then clam up as everything we are trying to process and express gets stuck in a bottleneck trying to get in and out. We are not silent and taciturn; the noise in here can be deafening.

Linked to empathy is the question of whether we as autistic people can manage social imagining; anticipating and preempting the feelings and responses of others. Of course we can. Sometimes we get it wrong but that doesn't mean we cannot do it. Some have more difficulty with it than others and sometimes we have to do it in different ways which are not always as reliable. We may not be so good at picking up non-verbal cues accurately; we may have to rely on experience and our memory of how people have reacted to similar things in the past. This can make us too cautious; it can make us seem to dwell on the past because we need it as a guide to help fill in some of the information a non autistic person can get more easily and up to date from the present.

I have personal experience of how the low self esteem and loneliness resulting from many misunderstandings and disconnections as a young undiagnosed autistic person can lead to addiction. As a 20 year old student I became addicted to gambling. At that time it was fruit machines, or puggies as they get called in Scotland; in my 30s I had a brief relapse involving scratchcards. Both times it was the same psychology behind it; I craved the adrenalin rush, the ego boost of winning and the popularity I thought I could buy with a windfall. I wanted to be able to tell a story about being a winner, reinforcing it by treating people to a drink or a meal or buying a box of biscuits for friends and flatmates. In my 30s I wanted to win big and have some charity in my beloved Highlands forever grateful to me for handing it over. Being constantly tired, I wanted to be the hero the easy way! Given my track record of being too proud to ask for help, I was so lucky in that both times I realised I had a problem before it was too late to sort it out on my own. I told myself that I wasn't addicted because I wasn't going into debt or stealing, but I was spending money I should have kept in my savings or used more constructively. Fortunately I also had my love of train journeys; once I had cancelled plans a few times because I ran out of money, I faced the fact that I was addicted and needed to stop. I wrote lists of other things I could do with specific amounts I was spending on gambling and made sure I put that money aside each time I was tempted, so that it was there as a tangible reminder that I still had it instead of it being in a puggie's guts or a newsagent's lottery counter till. I still have to be careful; I no longer have the daily temptation but I know that in a certain combination of circumstances I could still potentially relapse. I even have to be cautious bidding on eBay because although that isn't gambling as such, I can be drawn in to bidding more than I intend or should because I cannot bear to be seen to lose.

Beating an addiction is a major achievement but it is only part of the battle; the war is ongoing against the deeper issues behind that addiction. It is vital that we help each other by remembering to notice, encourage and praise the small victories which can build us up to be stronger, happier people; we also need to learn to acknowledge our own day to day results because often we are the only ones who can see them.

Feelings and Emotions

A key fact which we and those supporting us need to acknowledge and allow for is that autistic people can feel emotions with a greatly increased intensity. This in turn can cause problems as we struggle to deal with the overload and cope when things go wrong.

Autism is a developmental condition and although many autistic people can lead just as productive and varied, responsible adult lives as anyone else, we can retain certain difficulties and vulnerabilities like those experienced in childhood and adolescence when it comes to coping with intense emotion. This does not mean we are immature or childish people. It means that we have heightened sensitivity and feelings which become stronger as we grow.

If your feelings and emotions are becoming so difficult and painful that you are thinking about suicide or harming yourself or someone else, you must seek help immediately from a professional or someone you trust. You can contact The Samaritans by letter, email or telephone; in some areas there is a face to face drop-in service at specific opening times. You can talk to your doctor or any other doctor available to see you urgently; you can also call NHS 24 in a mental health crisis just as you can in a physical one. The number is now 111 and it is free to call from land lines and mobiles. Someone else can make the call for you if you are too distressed. Contact details for The Samaritans are provided in the final chapter.

It is useful to learn relaxation and breathing techniques to help you cope when emotions are becoming too strong, especially panic, anxiety or anger. Concentrating on your breathing, posture and heart rate can help you to deal with a crisis by focusing everything on being safe and grounded in the moment, taking on only the immediate need to get through moment by moment until your feelings return to a level you can cope with. This is similar to the principles of mindfulness. It is also something you can learn to do discreetly when outside; returning your breathing to normal and paying attention to your posture so that you give yourself a better chance to cope and to avoid the wrong kind of attention in a public place.

If you do find yourself overwhelmed by upsetting thoughts or feelings while you are out, it is important that you get to a safe place, and that you keep yourself safe while getting there. Remind yourself that you need to stay aware of dangers around you such as traffic. Make it part of your emergency coping plan to slow your breathing and to walk calmly. It may be difficult to do when your feelings are running high, but making yourself do it can be a useful distraction and diffusion technique. It also helps you to keep safe and avoid adding to your distress by people noticing your emotional state and making unhelpful comments, imposing unwanted interaction on you or taking advantage of you.

Recognising the kind of thought patterns which can spiral into a crisis is useful as you can take action before things get too bad. Remembering past events or imagining bad things which haven't actually happened are the kind of thoughts you can learn to recognise and distract yourself from. You might find it helpful to decide on a particular command to give yourself; something simple and meaningful like "NO: I am stopping this thought now". Think the words if you are outside; when alone you can either think them or say them.

Learn to recognise when you are thinking too much over and over about something which you cannot change because it is out of your control or in the past. This is ruminating and many autistic people tend to do it a lot. It is natural to remember things which affect you strongly; it can help to think about them if you can learn and plan different approaches in future but once that is all done and thinking about it only upsets you, it becomes a bad thing. At the same time, don't feel bad or guilty about thoughts coming into your mind. People end up very stressed when they become too strict about thoughts. Stopping a thought is not a simple choice; there is no physical barrier we can put up or place we can go to or avoid or habit we can decide to give up. What you should be aiming for is to keep getting better at pushing them away before they make you really upset.

Having a few options to distract yourself with something you genuinely enjoy and will engage with is another very helpful technique. Physical activity is good but you need to do something which will also occupy your thoughts; do puzzles, learn a language or look up something you are interested in online or in a book. Creative expression by writing, drawing, music or whatever you like to do can also help to refocus your mind.

If you need to vent anger, make sure you do so safely and in a way which will not get you into trouble. Vigorous exercise or punching something soft like a rolled up duvet, where you will not hurt yourself or damage property, can help as long as you don't do it for too long. If you write or draw something about your anger towards a person, make sure it is destroyed or kept where nobody else can find it. If you find that you keep looking at it and getting angry all over again, then it is no longer helpful and you should get rid of it.

Another thing you need to be cautious about is who you talk to about your feelings and emotions. Make sure it is someone you know you can trust, not a stranger who just happens to be there and seems sympathetic or someone you only know online. This is one of the most important reasons not to react to intense emotion by going out and getting drunk. Your judgement and inhibitions do not stay at the levels you need to stay safe when combining too much drink with strong emotion, even when the emotion is positive. You should also be wary if someone seems too keen to say bad things about other people or tell stories about their faults. Sympathising with your bad experience and agreeing with you about others' negative actions is one thing, but if they seem to only want to talk about people in a negative way, criticising the person more than the behaviour and not saying many positive things, they may just be gossiping. People who do this a lot may eventually say things about you to other people or repeat and exaggerate things you tell them.

Losing someone

The loss of someone from our lives, whether by death, moving away or choosing to end any kind of relationship, can be one of the hardest things for autistic people to deal with. This can be enhanced as time goes on because we feel the sympathy and support of others is getting less, just as the fatigue of long term grieving seems to get harder. Finding autism aware support is particularly important when dealing with issues like this.

The importance of acknowledging and allowing for the intense nature of autistic emotion has already been mentioned; another very important point is to remember how the autistic brain works. This can in itself be some comfort at difficult times; being able to understand what you are dealing with and apply your practical knowledge helps to bring a sense of returning control. Thought patterns and feelings in many autistic people are extremely rigid and long lasting. An autistic person does not "get over it" or "move on" in the same way or the same timescale as many non autistic people seem to. Changing thought patterns is a lot more complex and takes a lot longer; changing routines to reduce reminders or encounters with a lost relationship causes a whole extra set of stress reactions because of the importance of familiarity and routine. The rest of the world becomes less safe and familiar just when the autistic person needs safety and familiarity most. The truth is that nobody has the right to put a time limit on how long another person, autistic or not, should take to process a loss or intense disappointment. As an autistic person, you need and deserve all of the compassion, help and support you can get, even - indeed especially - when you are least able to engage with it.

You will have to be prepared for the fact that some people will never fully understand the extent and duration of some of your feelings. They may seem to be hard or uncaring or to have lost interest but really just not know how to help. They may have tried everything they can think of to help you feel better and not know what to say any more, or they may be afraid of saying the wrong thing and upsetting you more. It is hard to do but try to make sure you don't neglect everything else you have in common with these people; don't let your friendships and relationships wither away because of the one thing they cannot help you resolve.

It is very important to keep persevering with everything else you enjoy in life, even though for a time it will not feel the same as your grief is the strongest thing you are feeling. Hold onto the parts of your familiar routine which don't involve or remind you of the person, though at first it may seem as though everything does. Even though they won't seem exciting, you really need to slow down, convalesce and heal for a time. Think of it as an investment; the time will come when you find it easier and the good days happen more often. It doesn't mean you will forget. It just means you will feel more able to cope.

If you are struggling with the loss of a friendship or relationship, including one you never had but wished for, it can be very hard knowing that the person you are missing so much is friends or partners with someone else. It may be a while before this thought is any comfort but whatever relationships they have with anyone else, those people are not experiencing what you would have. Every relationship is unique; nobody can ever have the same relationship with your desired friend or partner as yours would have been. Your feelings are your own; they belong to you, not to anyone else.

You must look after your mental health and especially keep well clear of any behaviour patterns which could get you into trouble. No good can come of you upsetting yourself by looking at a lost friend or partner's Facebook page, reading their blog or looking for any information about them. If you keep trying to contact them, hang around places where they will be or do anything to try to get back at them for hurting you, then not only will you make yourself feel worse and put the time you start to feel better a lot further away, you could also find yourself in trouble with the police. You will end up feeling so bad about yourself it will be difficult for you to relate to anyone.

Even if you are still in contact with the person and on friendly terms, it is best to keep contact to a minimum until you start to feel stronger. Ask yourself before every text, email, phone call or going somewhere they will be, whether you are doing it for the right reasons. If you are doing it just for the sake of contact with them and it is unnecessary or there is an alternative, don't do it. You will have to be very honest with yourself. If you have a work or professional relationship, keep emotion and anything personal out of your communications with them. If you have to contact them, think carefully about everything you say. If you would not feel comfortable with their colleagues, partner or your own friends, boss or support workers seeing or hearing it, leave it out. If you are texting, messaging or emailing them socially, read over what you have written and imagine showing it to your most no-nonsense, straight talking friend or support worker. You do not have to actually show them; just imagine from your knowledge of them what they would be likely to say if they read it. If you feel uncomfortable with that thought, reword your message until you have something you would not be afraid to show them. If someone has asked you not to contact them, it is vital that you respect that. Not replying more than two or three times in a row should be treated in the same way as an explicit request not to contact. No feelings of sadness, boredom or emptiness are as bad as how it will feel if you not only push them so far they turn against you, but also get yourself into trouble for harassment.

If you are grieving for a person or a pet who has died, keep your photos, memories and keepsakes of them somewhere safe where you will not see them all the time but where you can look at them when you feel ready. Happy memories will eventually take over from the sadness. If it is a pet, this is another kind of grief which not everyone you know will necessarily understand especially as time goes on. All they need to understand is that you are grieving. The therapeutic bond many autistic people have with animals is vital and something for which you will always have a richer life.

Intensity, emptiness and addiction

Very often autistic people feel that life just doesn't match up to the intense emotional experience we crave. This coupled with our rigidity of thought and tendency to crave familiar routines at the same time as we seek that excitement can be a big part of why we end up in some of the relationship mourning situations already mentioned, or in destructive relationships of all kinds, or battling addictions.

You might think of addiction as only involving doing illegal or obviously dangerous things which you would never want to do. Addiction is more complicated than that and can happen very gradually. You need to be able to recognise certain signs and then have the courage and willpower to do something about it. If you are spending so much time doing something that you neglect other things and people in your life, it could be an addiction. If you are spending too much money, hiding how much you are doing something or not stopping for important things like eating, sleeping and washing, these are strong warnings of addiction. If you don't really enjoy it any more but cannot stop, that is addiction.

If you recognise that you have become or are becoming addicted to something such as spending, gambling, alcohol, drugs (including “legal highs” and prescribed medication in the wrong doses), computer games, sexual behaviours, fixating on someone or risk taking, seek help as soon as possible. Stay away from people and places around which you are most vulnerable; where you are most likely to be tempted or to get access to what you are addicted to. You will need willpower and it will be hard work, but there are things you can do and think about to get something positive from your situation. Try to think about why you have become so dependent on your addiction; why did you first get involved with it, even before you became addicted? Why did it make you feel good or better or comforted? If you can work out what you were getting or looking for from it, such as an escape, something familiar to do or a kind of interaction you feel is missing from your life, you can use that knowledge to start looking for a more constructive, balanced way of meeting that need without causing yourself the problems which come with addiction.

You can use your autistic traits to help you beat an addiction. Use rigidity of thought for determination to break the destructive habit, use desire to get things right for incentive to stop doing something which, even if legal, is harmful. Turn your intense emotions towards the things you used to enjoy which you have begun to neglect in favour of your growing addiction; think how good it will feel to be free. It can be done. Start today.

There are habits we can get into which fall short of addiction but still do us more harm than good. For instance, some people overeat to compensate for boredom and fatigue, feel comforted or fill an emotional or sensory void. This can become a way of life and make the person unhealthy and overweight. This makes them more tired, lowers self esteem and worsens the problems which tempted them to overeat in the first place. An effective way of tackling this is to remember what food is actually for. It is fuel for the body, not for the emotions. That doesn't mean you shouldn't enjoy your meals; just make healthier choices based on what your body needs, not your mood. A simple technique for reframing the way you look at food is to get into the habit of saying grace before meals. You do not have to follow any particular religion; just decide on something to say which gives thanks for the food you eat and the good health it brings you. If you are eating out or with other people, you might prefer to think the words rather than saying them out loud; it will work just as well.

Dieting advice is specific to each individual's needs and should come from a doctor; you may consider asking for a referral to a dietician. Planning healthy meals, keeping a record of how much you eat (remember to include all you drink as well), only buying what you need and getting the help of your support network as well as the cooperation of anyone who shares places where you store food are all positive life skills which will make you feel better for taking control and responsibility.

Chapter 12: Supporting Someone Else

This is something I try my best to do; I care very much and am more likely to be assertive on behalf of someone else than of myself. I freely admit that I am not an easy person to support. I have a lot of trust issues and will always err on the side of caution, or as some people have put it, can turn anything negative! I allow bad experiences to influence how I take the input of completely different and unrelated people. Of course I also feel I have to get everything perfect; on my own initiative, not as a result of someone else's instruction otherwise I feel that I am doing the work and they are getting the credit. Nobody actually gets to do that. I know that my ideals are unrealistic; we all need support, guidance and the benefit of others' experience sometimes.

I also appreciate that people genuinely want to reach out and help but don't always know how best to go about it. There is a deep seated reluctance in many people to ask the person they are trying to support; they feel it will add to the person's stress, or look unprofessional or undermine their position if they are giving the support in an official capacity. We all need to ask questions more; the person needing support can find that helpful in its own right as it enables a process of building trust and understanding their own needs better. I hope that writing these tips from my point of view as an autistic person can go some way towards breaking down some of the obstacles which I acknowledge I have had a big part in creating with regard to my own support network.

It is important for everyone, autistic or not, to remember that sometimes the people who appear strongest need help the most. Several years ago a close friend put a sad face as her Facebook status. I was taken aback; I knew that for this particular friend to do that, something had to be badly wrong. She was online so I opened a private chat and over the next couple of hours I had my eyes well and truly opened about the pressure she had been feeling. Because she always presented as upbeat and put witty, colourful status updates online, everyone including me had taken that at face value and unwittingly added to the pressure by telling her how much her statuses were valued as an antidote to some of the drama and drivel going about. We were all genuinely complimenting her with no expectation attached, but she felt that she would be letting people down if she revealed how she was feeling. She was afraid that people would change towards her if she showed vulnerability. After checking on her later that day, we never spoke of the conversation again. She may or may not recognise herself if she reads this. I just hope that by not mentioning it again, I have given her the reassurance of seeing that the changes she feared didn't happen while at the same time knowing I am here if she ever needs me.

I am forever grateful to my best friend Matthew, who is on my wavelength and can appreciate the humour I frequently use as a coping mechanism while at the same time never losing sight of what it really is. Too many people have seen my humour and thought that is all there is to me, or all they want or need to bother engaging with. Matthew completely gets and thoroughly enjoys my sense of humour but he also knows when to take me seriously; to listen and give me the extra time I need. I am also grateful to all those who hang in there during the tough times and keep on trying, not only for me but for all of us with our diverse needs. Continuing to learn from each other and reach out, even more than the times when things go smoothly, is how we know we can still make it.

Supporting Someone Else

This chapter is mainly for anyone supporting an autistic person in life, whether personally or professionally; it is also of interest to autistic people supporting anyone else, autistic or not, and struggling to cope because of too much empathy or difficulty maintaining healthy boundaries.

Read up about autism if your knowledge and experience is limited. Autistic people's needs and profile of difficulties and strengths varies a lot from individual to individual but there are many common traits. Where possible read what autistic people have written.

Be aware that an autistic person may find some habits very distracting; try to avoid doing things like tapping, pen clicking or eating (unless you have arranged to meet the person specifically to go and eat).

When trying to offer support to someone who is under stress or very upset about something, it can be difficult to process and correctly interpret their responses. A person's tone of voice can be affected by stress, making them sound offhand or hostile. If you take offence, communication and trust can take some work to restore; the person when already under stress is likely to be hugely demoralised by yet another misunderstanding in an area which is consistently difficult for them to navigate. Give them the benefit of the doubt and the time to realise and modify their tone. If their manner becomes intimidating or aggressive, keep calm and gently alert them to how they are coming across. Let them know that you want to help and are speaking out of concern.

Actual or threatened physical aggression is a different matter. You are never obliged to tolerate that and must get out of the situation; if you can, take away anything the person may use to do harm and get someone else to come with you when you return to them after a cooling off period.

Sustained mental aggression including manipulation and emotional blackmail should not be tolerated either and you should seek advice if you feel that this is happening. Emotional blackmail is trying to get someone to do something they don't want to do, cannot or should not do by saying things to make them feel guilty or worried. An example of this could be if you are only free and comfortable having telephone conversations or meeting with someone to help them through a problem twice a week and they start asking you to be available more often. If you have explained to them that you are already doing all you can and they tell you they might harm themselves or someone else if you don't increase your contact with them, this threat is emotional blackmail.

It can be easy to fall into the trap of thinking that to give effective support, you have to know what someone needs without having to be told. Although you will have more idea as you get to know someone, don't be afraid to ask them questions about what they need and how you can help them most effectively. Ask them what they need you to do; keep the pace of the conversation gentle and avoid giving too many choices or asking too many questions too quickly.

When you do ask questions, allow them time and space to answer you. Autistic people under stress will often need more time than usual to process questions and to frame answers. Silence can be a desperately needed refuge and vital space. Prompting them will increase their stress.

Acknowledge the particular nature of autistic thinking, both to the person and to yourself. Set, established thought patterns and processes are very difficult to change or even to see differently. This can appear as stubbornness or as rejection of your reasoning; it can be frustrating, especially if they eventually do see things differently but present it as a new idea or an insight from someone else. It may be that someone else was lucky with their timing or just happened to put it in a slightly different way which resonated with the person. It is not a reflection on you. They may even feel the need to believe it is their own insight because it is the only way they can allow themselves to feel better; hearing it from someone else may feel like being told they are wrong therefore not deserving to let it help them. Getting things right, rewards and pleasing people can be the earliest system a bewildered, overloaded and often bullied autistic child understands and brings with them from those formative years; this perceived lifeline retains its hold and significance well into adulthood, sometimes for the rest of their life.

Expect to cover the same ground more than once; be patient and don't rebuke an autistic person for repetition or try to make the conversation more dynamic and interesting by saying "we've already had this conversation" or similar irritated phrases. If something is genuinely becoming an obsession and obviously harming the person, try to divert them to something more constructive and then let them see how much better that makes them feel. Make sure that any challenge of repetition or being in a rut is for the benefit of the person, not because you are bored of the subject.

Always let the person you are supporting take the lead with regard to humour. Seeing the funny side of problems can be a very effective coping strategy and beneficial to their health but it has to come from them and it cannot be rushed; if they feel you are laughing at them or trivialising their feelings, it will damage their trust.

Be aware of your own boundaries and the limits of what you can do. Make it clear from the start that you don't have all the answers; if you are only available at particular times, make sure that they understand this and keep to those times. It is never healthy for anyone to be reliant upon one person; keep taking an interest in their other outlets and support network and encouraging them to use them. A balance between self reliance and a network of support sources is much better for their self esteem as well as your ability to stay strong enough to support others effectively.

If you are becoming seriously concerned that the person you are supporting may harm themselves or anyone else, do not be forced into agreeing secrecy. Encourage them strongly to seek proper trained help; ask them to tell you who they would like you to contact if their distress is going beyond what you can manage. Be honest about your limits and seek help and support for yourself if you need to. This is not a betrayal; it is crisis management and protecting yourself, which you are entitled to do. It is taking responsibility for yourself, which is just what you are encouraging the person to do. You can still support them to access and engage with that further help they need and you can still be there for them as they come through it.

If you do feel that someone is becoming too reliant on you, approach them gently and tactfully with your concerns. Do not let resentment build up and end up suddenly snapping at them. This will make you feel awful and could be a devastating blow completely out of the blue to them. Keep reminding them of their other support options, the importance of using all their options and of their own part in making progress; why it is so much better for them that they don't rely too much on you or any one source of support.

Be aware of the risks of co-dependency. It is good to feel needed and to know you are making a difference to someone, but this can sometimes become counterproductive without the person giving support being aware of it. Let the person grow; encourage them to do more for themselves in small, manageable steps as they become more confident, rather than automatically giving the same level of help even as they are managing better. Take it as a very positive achievement rather than a rejection if they come to need you less; let them know you will be there for them if their needs change in the future.

Always encourage the person to be actively involved in looking for ways to make things better for themselves; to try to think of solutions before asking for help and to plan out what goals they want to achieve and how. Praise and encourage them frequently; let them process and enjoy achievements and milestones before suggesting any new challenge, or they may end up feeling that they can never be good enough to please you.

When choosing or suggesting a place to meet, consider the other person's sensory needs; how bright, busy, noisy, cluttered or pervaded by strong smells any venue is likely to be. What causes difficulty for one autistic person may not be perceived as a significant problem by another; remember what you know of the person's needs and be prepared to change venues if they begin to struggle. They may be too polite or too stressed to tell you so you will need to watch for signs of discomfort. Keep in mind that a place you find quiet and suitable during the week may be completely different at the weekend, for instance anywhere which has live music or shows sports on TV. Pay attention to the person's pattern of needs; if for instance they feel safer sitting near the door or if they find side by side easier than face to face. Check whether any special events are scheduled which will cause disruption or bring extra crowds.

If you need to change or cancel arrangements to meet the person, especially at short notice, handle the change sensitively. We all know that things can crop up unexpectedly; it is equally inevitable that autistic people will find these unexpected changes stressful, however unavoidable they are and whatever the circumstances. An autistic person may struggle to react appropriately, especially on first learning of the change. This is not them being bad, unreasonable or selfish. It is a part of their condition. Never criticise them for finding it difficult or for showing stress, or use lifestyle differences to chastise them (such as "you would understand if you had children / were working"). Acknowledge that it is difficult for them and that you are sorry; this is an expression of compassion and empathy, not an apology for your legitimate need to change your plans. Offer to reschedule but accept that this may be too much for the person to think about immediately; let them know when you will be in touch or when they can contact you.

If talking about sensitive subjects with someone in a public place or anywhere there are other people around, pay attention to any risk of the conversation being overheard, especially if people's names are being mentioned or anything confidential is involved. Autistic people can have difficulty judging volume as well as tone of voice and may also speak more loudly to compensate for heightened sensory input and difficulty filtering out ambient sound. We don't always realise we are doing it, especially if the background noise increases and decreases.

Be prepared for the fact you may never get much feedback on how the person gets on in the future; you may never know how much of a difference you made. Even if little or nothing seems to have changed, it may just be taking that extra time autistic people need to process things. If nothing else, the fact you cared, reached out into their world and tried to meet and help them there them means a lot.

Sources of Further Help and Support

The value of autism specific support services such as the one stop shops managed by Autism Initiatives, Scottish Autism, the National Autistic Society and similar organisations cannot be overstated. Fully autism aware and trained staff can give support themselves and also help service users to get the most out of the support available from more general services. It is not just about the support itself being autism aware; it is making the environment in which it is given autism friendly through awareness of sensory, social and communication needs. Autism services provide a focal point for making connections and establishing links with the best of proven autism friendly service in other organisations, whether by referrals or through becoming aware of service users' experiences and recommendations as well as learning of areas where things could be done better and helping to facilitate this. The opportunity to share experiences with other autistic people can have huge benefits as it is so helpful to know you are not alone and get moral support and knowing praise in your daily battles.

If there is a one stop shop in your area, try to make use of it as much as possible. Look up autism support and the name of your nearest big town or city, or ask at your local doctor's surgery, council service point, library, Citizens' Advice Bureau or similar organisation. You do not necessarily have to attend in person every time you need support; there will be options to make contact by telephone, email or letter and there may be a newsletter you can ask them to send you or a social networking presence such as a Twitter feed or Facebook page you can follow.

Local self help, support or user groups for autistic people and / or their families and carers are a very useful source of contacts and solidarity. Getting involved with these as a member or volunteer can give an added sense of purpose and help the groups to continue helping others, as they are often run by a dedicated but very small core of people who have a lot to do.

Crisis support

If you need to talk to someone about difficult feelings, including thoughts of suicide, The Samaritans offer several different ways of contacting them. You do not have to be suicidal; they will help anyone who needs to reach out.

Telephone (the quickest way to make contact): 116 123. This number is free to call from mobiles and land lines and will not appear on telephone bills.

Post: Chris, Freepost RSRB-KKBY-CYJK, PO Box 9090, Stirling FK8 2SA (please include your address so that someone can reply; your letter will be shredded to protect confidentiality once a volunteer has responded. They aim to respond within seven days.)

Email: jo@samaritans.org

Contact information taken from www.samaritans.org. Chris and Jo are pen names to preserve the anonymity of the volunteers.

At the time of writing this book, The Samaritans are in the process of developing text and online contact options with a quicker response time than the post and email options. Please keep checking their website if this interests you.

NHS 24

The out of hours number is free to call and is now 111. This has changed from the old 0845 number to make it easier and clearer for people. It is only for use should you or someone else be unwell and unable to wait until the doctor's surgery opens. For life threatening emergencies you should still call 999. You can also access online help and advice via www.nhs24.com.

Autism specific information and resources

Autism Initiatives UK uses a positive, person centred approach to helping autistic people, with an emphasis on involving the person and focusing on making their autistic traits work in their favour.

Autism Initiatives Head Office contact details:

Telephone: 0151 330 9500 (office hours)

Post: 7 Chesterfield Road, Liverpool L23 9XL

Email: info@autisminitiatives.org

Website: www.autisminitiatives.org

The National Autistic Society (NAS) has information and advice on a wide range of topics, specifically tailored for autistic people and those helping them.

NAS Autism Helpline: 0808 800 4104 (10am-4pm Monday to Friday except bank holidays; free to call from land lines and most mobile networks)

Postal enquiries: Autism Helpline, National Autistic Society, 393 City Road, London EC1V 1NG (they aim to reply within 14 days of receiving letters)

There is an online enquiry option via the website: www.autism.org.uk.

Citizens' Advice Bureau

Contact details will depend on where you live. You can find your local office and its contact details and opening times on www.citizensadvice.org.uk.

Bullying

National Bullying Helpline:

Telephone: 0845 22 55 787

Post: PO Box 1276, Swindon SN25 4UX

Email: info@nationalbullyinghelpline.co.uk

Website: www.nationalbullyinghelpline.co.uk

Online message boards for autistic people

asperclick.com

www.asd-forum.org.uk

www.aspievillage.org.uk

These and similar online communities can be a source of support and useful information as well as advice from the experiences of other autistic people. Remember that the people who post on these message boards are not trained counsellors or advisers. Some posts can appear very blunt; intense emotional expression and arguments can unfold. Read with caution as there may be triggers which could upset you. Be careful about disclosing any sensitive information and do not give out your personal details, or go alone to meet anyone you get to know on any online forum.

All details correct at the time of publication.

Acknowledgements

Special thanks to:

Richard Ibbotson, former National Director of Autism Initiatives Scotland, and Deputy Director Catherine Steedman who saw the potential for this book and encouraged its completion.

David Morrison at PublishNation who made it possible.

Faith Wilson, who as well as providing invaluable additional material for the chapter on travelling has been a consistent friend, colleague and mentor, always believing in me.

Arlene Johnstone; for inspiring much needed change in my life. #YouRock!

Jeni Miller; here's to many more excellent adventures and bogus journeys.

Matthew Day, my best friend, for everything. I couldn't do any of this without you, bro.

Love and light to:

My fellow service users and volunteers at Albion House: Respect, peace and strength.

InverGill, Kirsten, Andrew, Angela and the aforementioned Jeni and Faith: Team Albion!

Jill, Claire, Julie, Chris and all my Perth friends at Number 3: A bond I will always treasure.

All at Number 6 in Edinburgh: Where it began for me.

The Highland One Stop Shop Advisory Group: For letting me in, eventually!

The CHANGE event planning group: For the ongoing journey; Fiona, for keeping the lines open!; Alison and Karen, 'til we three meet again.

AvieGill and all at the Strathspey Railway: For supporting and enabling me to sustain both my voluntary office jobs and still complete this project.

Flora, Mike, Mitzi, Matilda, Mischa, Marie, Max and Suzi: For being my Aviemore family.

Ann, Ruth, Karen, Catalina, Bridget, Gabi, Mark, Kabie: For conversation and inspiration.

Jean-Pierre: For being an honest and courageous friend to this Highlander through the best and the worst; keeping me alert, never complacent and certainly never bored!

Proceeds from the sale of this book will go to support the ongoing work of the Highland One Stop Shop.

Email: highlandoss@aiscotland.org.uk

Website: highlandoss.org.uk

Autism Initiatives Scotland Head Office: 11 Granton Square, Edinburgh EH5 1HX

Tel: 0131 551 7260

Email hos@aiscotland.org.uk.